# CLARENCE P. HORNUNG

# *100 Great Antique Automobiles*

## IN FULL-COLOR PRINTS

WITH AN INTRODUCTION BY JOHN BELL RAE
AND NOTES ON THE PLATES BY JAMES J. BRADLEY

DOVER PUBLICATIONS, INC.
*New York*

*To the gallant pathfinders*
*whose early experiments*
*in self-propulsion*
*left an enduring testament*
*for all America*
*to share and enjoy*

Copyright © 1991 by Dover Publications, Inc.
All rights reserved under Pan American and International Copyright Conventions.

Published in Canada by General Publishing Company, Ltd., 30 Lesmill Road, Don Mills, Toronto, Ontario.

Published in the United Kingdom by Constable and Company, Ltd., 3 The Lanchesters, 162–164 Fulham Palace Road, London W6 9ER.

This Dover edition, first published in 1991, is a republication, in a new format and typographically reset, of *Portrait Gallery of Early Automobiles*, originally published by Harry N. Abrams, Inc., New York, in 1968. The four brief part introductions and the frontispiece have been omitted. All 100 plates were first published, in large portfolio format, as *Gallery of the American Automobile* by Collectors' Prints, Inc., New York, in 1965.

Manufactured in the United States of America
Dover Publications, Inc., 31 East 2nd Street, Mineola, N.Y. 11501

*Library of Congress Cataloging-in-Publication Data*

Hornung, Clarence Pearson.
    100 great antique automobiles in full-color prints / Clarence P. Hornung ; with an introduction by John Bell Rae and notes on the plates by James J. Bradley.
        p.    cm.
    Includes index.
    ISBN 0-486-26841-1 (pbk.)
    1. Automobiles—History.   2. Antique and classic cars—Pictorial works.
    I. Title.   II. Title: One hundred great antique automobiles in full-color prints.
TL15.H57   1991
629.222'022'2—dc20                                          91-17963
                                                                 CIP

# *Contents*

| | |
|---|---|
| Foreword, by Clarence P. Hornung | v |
| Introduction, by John Bell Rae | vii |
| | PLATES |
| Dudgeon Steam Wagon, 1853 | 1 |
| Roper Steam Carriage, 1863 | 2 |
| Carhart Steam Wagon, 1871 | 3 |
| Selden Road Wagon, 1877 | 4 |
| Copeland Steam Tricycle, 1886 | 5 |
| Morrison-Sturgis Electric, 1890 | 6 |
| Nadig Road Wagon, 1891 | 7 |
| Lambert Gasoline Buggy, 1891 | 8 |
| Schloemer-Toepfer Carriage, 1892 | 9 |
| Duryea Gasoline Buggy, 1893 | 10 |
| Black Gasoline Carriage, 1893 | 11 |
| Haynes Gasoline Carriage, 1894 | 12 |
| Morris & Salom Electrobat, 1895 | 13 |
| Holtzer-Cabot Electric, 1895 | 14 |
| Duryea Motor Wagon, 1895 | 15 |
| Ford Quadricycle, 1896 | 16 |
| King Horseless Carriage, 1896 | 17 |
| Mueller Motor Carriage, 1897 | 18 |
| Olds Motor Carriage, 1897 | 19 |
| Autocar Phaeton, 1898 | 20 |
| Woods Electric Hansom, 1898 | 21 |
| Ford Gasoline Carriage, 1898 | 22 |
| Winton Motor Carriage, 1898 | 23 |
| Riker Electric Tricycle, 1898 | 24 |
| Packard Model "A", 1899 | 25 |
| Columbia Daumon Victoria, 1899 | 26 |
| Locomobile Steamer, 1899 | 27 |
| Knox Three-Wheeler, 1899 | 28 |
| Riker Electric Brougham, 1900 | 29 |
| Woods Station Wagon, 1900 | 30 |
| Columbia Electric Phaeton, 1900 | 31 |
| Haynes-Apperson Surrey, 1901 | 32 |
| Riker Theater Bus, 1901 | 33 |
| White Steamer, 1901 | 34 |
| Duryea Phaeton, 1902 | 35 |
| Packard "F" Tonneau, 1902 | 36 |
| Franklin Runabout, 1902 | 37 |
| Rambler Runabout, 1902 | 38 |
| Stanley Steamer, 1902 | 39 |
| Studebaker Electric Runabout, 1902 | 40 |
| Winton Touring Car, 1903 | 41 |
| Peerless Touring Car, 1903 | 42 |
| Cadillac Tonneau, 1903 | 43 |
| Ford "A" Tonneau, 1903 | 44 |
| Oldsmobile Curved Dash Runabout, 1903 | 45 |
| Locomobile Tonneau De Luxe, 1904 | 46 |
| Rambler Tonneau, 1904 | 47 |
| Studebaker Touring Car, 1904 | 48 |
| Ford "B" Touring Car, 1905 | 49 |
| Holsman Surrey, 1905 | 50 |
| Cadillac "D" Touring Car, 1905 | 51 |
| Stearns Limousine "40–45", 1906 | 52 |
| Ford "K" Touring Car, 1906 | 53 |
| Autocar Runabout, 1906 | 54 |
| Marmon "D" Touring Car, 1906 | 55 |
| Packard "S-24" Victoria, 1906 | 56 |
| Cadillac "M" Touring Car, 1906 | 57 |
| Maxwell Tourabout, 1907 | 58 |
| Apperson Touring Car, 1907 | 59 |
| Buick "G" Runabout, 1907 | 60 |
| Pope-Waverley "60-A" Surrey, 1907 | 61 |
| Cadillac "H" Limousine, 1907 | 62 |
| Oldsmobile "A" Touring Car, 1907 | 63 |
| S. & M. Simplex Limousine, 1907 | 64 |
| Pierce Great Arrow Touring Car, 1908 | 65 |
| Rauch & Lang Brougham, 1908 | 66 |
| Stanley Roadster, 1908 | 67 |

Ford Model "T" Touring Car, 1909     68

Studebaker "A" Suburban, 1909     69

Knox "M" Limousine, 1909     70

Thomas Flyer Touring Car, 1909     71

Hudson Roadster, 1910     72

Chalmers-Detroit Coupé, 1910     73

Reo Roadster, 1910     74

Buick "10" Toy Tonneau, 1910     75

Packard Berline, 1910     76

Sears Motor Buggy, 1910     77

Oakland "K" Touring Car, 1910     78

Brewster Limousine, 1911     79

Alco Touring Car, 1911     80

Buick "26" Runabout, 1911     81

White "30" Landaulet, 1911     82

Matheson Toy Tonneau, 1911     83

Mercer Raceabout, 1911     84

Rambler Landaulet, 1911     85

Simplex Speedster, 1912     86

Abbott-Detroit "30" Roadster, 1912     87

Packard "30" Close-Coupled, 1912     88

Lozier Toy Tonneau, 1912     89

American "22-B" Roadster, 1913     90

Cadillac Coupé, 1913     91

Overland "69" Touring Car, 1913     92

Peerless Roadster, 1913     93

Chevrolet Royal Mail Roadster, 1914     94

Stutz Bearcat, 1914     95

Pierce-Arrow Vestibule Suburban, 1914     96

Chevrolet Baby Grand Touring Car, 1914     97

Hupmobile "32" Touring Car, 1914     98

Dodge Touring Car, 1914     99

Locomobile Town Coupé, 1915     100

Notes on the Plates, by James J. Bradley     xiii

Index     xxvii

# *Foreword to the 1968 Edition*

IN THIS VOLUME we examine the crude and quaint prototypes of motorcars built in the United States from 1853 to 1915. The sequence of plates starts with the earliest experimental efforts of pioneer machinists and continues well into the era of established manufacturing practices and techniques. Probing into the unexplored areas of automotive beginnings, the primary purpose of this study is to present new pictorial evidence both of antiquity and artistry. To portray adequately the progression from cumbersome steam wagon to sophisticated town car, our motorcade advances from before the Civil War to World War I, emphasizing along the route the comparative pattern of change and style trends of later years. Only those vehicles have been illustrated for which authentic documentation in the form of drawings, engravings or contemporary photographs were available.

Secondly, our aim has been to provide stimulation and inspiration by a sound portrayal of historic exemplars. The choice of one hundred subjects, especially those built after the turn of the century, has largely been governed by aesthetic considerations. Color has been freely introduced in the interest of variety and visual excitement. Purists may argue that such liberties violate the manufacturers' intentions, but what deadly monotony would result from following too rigidly the standard factory colors of black, blue, maroon and Brewster green.

How reminiscent this would be of Henry Ford's apocryphal remark: "The customer may have any color provided it is black."

All of the illustrations in this collection, together with the accompanying notes and comments, were issued originally in a monumental portfolio of art plates called *Gallery of the American Automobile*. Research, design and production on this project started back in 1950 and continued right up to the year of publication in 1965. An unprecedented undertaking, the work has entailed many thousands of sketches, finished drawings and color overlays. The acceptance of the finished work, issued in a limited edition, and its placement in key libraries and collectors' hands as a major reference tool, stamps the *Gallery* as a significant contribution to our industrial history.

Through the cooperation of the original publisher, Collectors' Prints, Inc., these plates have been made available as a basis for the present volume. It is my hope that this collection of pictures, previously available only to a limited few at great cost, will now reach a wider audience.

C.P.H.

*New York, N.Y.*

# Introduction

## By JOHN BELL RAE

THE STORY OF THE AMERICAN AUTOMOBILE has been told by many different people in many different ways, for the simple reason that it is a many-faceted story. It can be told in terms of a phenomenally rapid industrial growth with far-reaching effects on the American economy, or of the technological revolution that we call mass production, or of the development of mass mobility in a way that has transformed American society, or in a variety of other ways. Certainly the most colorful approach is through the cars themselves and the men who conceived and built them. It can be done in words, but it can be done much better with pictures, as Clarence Hornung has demonstrated in this volume.

The automobile is not an American invention. The idea of a mechanically propelled highway vehicle goes back to people like Roger Bacon and Leonardo da Vinci, but it was only with the advent of the steam engine that the dream could become a practical possibility. There is a long record of experiments with steam-powered road vehicles both in Europe and America. In the United States John Fitch made a model of a steam carriage about 1786 but then turned his attention to steamboats. Nathan Read, a Massachusetts lawyer and member of the faculty of Harvard College, experimented with the perennial problem of the weight-power ratio and obtained a patent in 1790 for a light-weight steam engine suitable for a carriage. But while drawings of the projected vehicle have survived, he never actually built one.

The first American to put a mechanically powered vehicle on the road was Oliver Evans. He seems to have had the idea as early as 1775, but it took him until 1805 to put it into operation. He did this with the *Orukter Amphibolos,* the "amphibious digger." It was a dredge for use in Philadelphia harbor, but Evans took the opportunity to demonstrate the feasibility of a steam carriage by mounting the dredge on a wagon, gearing the engine to the wheels, and driving the *Orukter* around the center of Philadelphia and then into the Schuylkill under its own power. Nevertheless, the Commonwealth of Pennsylvania still refused to let him put "steam waggons" on its highways. Thomas Blanchard of Springfield, Massachusetts, got a more favorable reception when he built an eight-passenger vehicle there in 1825. However, the steam engines of that day were too heavy and clumsy and consumed too much fuel for adaptation to a highway carriage.

The gradual improvement of the steam engine produced more intensive experimentation. An American named Richard Dudgeon first built a steam car in 1853, later exhibited in London, followed by a second in 1866–67. Two contemporaries, J. K. Fisher of New York and Perry Dickson of Erie, Pennsylvania, staged a bitter journalistic quarrel in 1865 over the merits of their respective vehicles. Dr. J. M. Carhart built a "steam buggy" in Racine, Wisconsin, in 1871, which stimulated the state legislature to offer a prize of $10,000 for a "cheap and practical substitute for the use of horses and other animals on the highway and farm." ($5,000 was awarded to a steam carriage that made the 200 miles from Green Bay to Madison in a week, in 1878. The legislature made a Solomonic judgment that while the vehicle worked all right, it was not a "cheap and practical substitute" for the horse.)

Most important of these experimenters was Sylvester Hayward Roper of Roxbury, Massachusetts, who built ten steam carriages between 1859 and 1895, and was even able to make money by exhibiting them at county fairs. Further commercial development was handicapped by the lack of good roads in the United States. Otherwise the Americans might have progressed beyond the promising development of steam omnibuses in Britain, which was abruptly cut off by the absurd "Red Flag" law of 1865, whereby any self-propelled vehicle on a public highway was limited to a speed of 4 mph and had to be preceded by a man on foot carrying a red flag. (The red flag requirement was rescinded in 1878, but the speed restriction remained in force until 1896.)

Before the steam engine had been refined to the point where it could be used in a practical automobile, two competitors appeared in the internal combustion engine and the electric motor. The latter had some strong advantages: it was clean and noiseless and required no complicated transmission. Its handicap was the limitation of the battery; an electric automobile was severely restricted in both speed and range. In the early days this did not matter very much because highway travel was predominantly local anyway, and the electric car enjoyed a very considerable vogue. The first American to build an electric automobile was William Morrison of Des Moines, Iowa, who ran his car in Chicago in 1890. He was followed by two Philadelphia engineers, Henry G. Morris and Pedro Salom, who built a car called the "Electrobat" in 1894. The motor came from General Electric. The Electrobat did well in the race sponsored by the *Chicago Times-Herald* in 1895, and Morris and Salom then launched the business operation which, in other hands, became the famous, or notorious, Electric Vehicle Company.

However, the mainstream of automobile history was to be the development of cars powered by the internal combustion engine. The gasoline automobile is clearly of European origin, with a long series of experiments culminating in the appearance of the first Benz and Daimler vehicles in Germany in 1886. The only possible American claimant to priority was George B. Selden, a patent attorney and inventor of Rochester, New York, who conceived plans for a "road engine" to be powered by an engine of the "liquid hydrocarbon variety." This was in 1877 and his patent application was filed on May 8, 1879. Selden, however, delayed having his patent issued until 1895, and no vehicle conforming to his specifications was built until 1905.

American experimentation followed close on the European achievement. Between 1888 and 1893 several gasoline-powered cars were actually run in the United States. Those for which there is a clear record are: a car built in 1891 by Henry Nadig, a machinist in

Allentown, Pennsylvania; one made by Gottfried Schloemer and Frank Toepfer in 1892; one built by Charles H. Black in Indianapolis in 1893; and a three-wheeled vehicle designed by John W. Lambert, in Ohio City, Ohio, in 1891. These, like the earlier steam cars, were all individually constructed in machine shops and home workshops. None led to any continuing and lasting development. Two claims can be rejected. Edward Joel Pennington alleged that he had completed a car in 1890, but Pennington was a glib promoter with a propensity for glowing pronouncements that somehow never materialized into operable automobiles. Henry Ford claimed that his first car was run in Detroit in 1892, but all the available evidence indicates that on this matter his memory was at fault.

The story of the American gasoline automobile begins effectively with two brothers, Charles E. and J. Frank Duryea. Charles was a bicycle mechanic and Frank a toolmaker, and they first became interested in making a car in 1889, when a description of a Benz was published in the *Scientific American*. They began work in 1891 on a design Charles thought up, with a free piston engine and a friction transmission. Charles left the project in his brother's hands a year later, and Frank completed the car after installing a completely new engine and transmission. The car was first driven in Springfield, Massachusetts, on September 21, 1893. A second Duryea car won distinction by being the only entrant to finish the course in the *Chicago Times-Herald* race, of 1895, and another ran in a road rally from London to Brighton, England, a year later to celebrate the repeal of the four-miles-an-hour restriction. The brothers were in business together briefly but separated in 1898. Charles engaged in a variety of activities connected with automobiles; Frank was the builder of the Stevens-Duryea car until he retired on grounds of ill health in 1915. He died in Madison, Connecticut, in 1967, aged 97.

The Duryea car ushered in the horseless carriage era of the American automobile. For the next ten years there was a sequence of experimental cars, most of them designed on the lines of the horse-drawn buggy but with an engine attached at some convenient place, usually under the driver's seat. Their designers were a widely assorted group of individuals, for the most part men with some technical training or experience but drawn from every segment of American life.

Close on the heels of the Duryeas was Elwood Haynes, a college-trained engineer who had to do a great deal of traveling as field superintendent of an Indiana oil company. He began to design a gasoline car in 1891, and his vehicle, built by Elmer and Edgar Apperson in their machine shop in Kokomo, Indiana, first ran on July 4, 1894. There was a Haynes-Apperson Company for a few years and then the two split. Next came Hiram Percy Maxim, a graduate of M.I.T., son of the inventor of the Maxim gun, and later himself the inventor of the Maxim silencer. He got his idea because he became tired of the effort of pushing a bicycle. He was, he says himself, "blissfully unaware" of the work of either the European or the American pioneers, but he arrived at the same solution to the problem and in 1895, after three years of trial and error, he mounted a gasoline engine on a Columbia tandem tricycle that he had bought for thirty dollars. His first trial run failed because he had not thought to provide a clutch for disconnecting the engine, but he overcame the difficulties and had an operable machine in 1895.

Maxim is a very important figure because his experiments attracted the attention of the Pope Manufacturing Company of Hartford, Connecticut, then the biggest manufacturers of bicycles in the United States. In due course Maxim went to Hartford to design motor vehicles for Pope—mainly electrics because Colonel Albert A. Pope believed, "You can't get people to sit over an explosion." The Pope venture began production in 1897 and turned out 500 electrics and about 40 gasoline cars in the next two years, using the same trade name of Columbia as was used for the firm's bicycles. This was the first large-scale production of American automobiles.

Three more pioneering efforts with gasoline cars appeared in 1896.

In Cleveland Alexander Winton, a brilliant but crotchety Scots engineer who had become a successful bicycle manufacturer, demonstrated a gasoline car in September, 1896. A year later he began commercial production of gasoline automobiles under the name of the Winton Motor Carriage Company. Meanwhile the horseless carriage had also arrived in Detroit, first in the form of a car designed by Charles Brady King, a Cornell-trained engineer and son of a United States Army officer. The vehicle was built in Lauer's Machine Shop and was first driven on Woodward Avenue, on March 6, 1896. King went on to have a distinguished career as an automotive and aeronautical engineer, but he never became important as a manufacturer of automobiles. The second car in Detroit was more historic. It was Henry Ford's "quadricycle," the first Ford car, built in the shed next to the rented house on Bagley Avenue where the Fords lived while Henry worked as chief engineer for the Detroit Edison Company. It was ready in June, 1896, but Ford discovered that he had to knock down part of the wall of the shed in order to get the contraption out on the street. A protesting landlord arrived on the scene and remained to help get the car going by pushing it. This was just a beginning. It would be several years yet before Henry Ford could become securely established in the automobile industry, but he was quite definitely one of the pioneer designers of a horseless carriage, even if he was not, as he himself and millions of other people later came to believe, the first.

Next on the list among important figures in the early development of the American automobile was Ransom Eli Olds. He was a partner with his father in the P. F. Olds & Son Co. manufacturing steam engines in Lansing, Michigan. Like so many other pioneers in both Europe and America, when he became interested in highway vehicles he experimented first with steam as the motive power. He built two steam cars, the first in 1887 followed by one in 1892, before he decided that the internal combustion engine offered better prospects. He had a workable gasoline car by 1897 and two years later was able to organize the Olds Motor Works and go into production. The company moved to Detroit and there, in March, 1901, suffered a disastrous fire that destroyed everything except a single one-cylinder curved-dash buggy which Olds had designed in the belief that there was a market for a low-priced car. This model became one of the most famous in automobile history: the "Merry Oldsmobile," the first car to be manufactured in thousands. At what seemed a peak of success Olds and his financial backers quarreled over company policy and Olds left, to find support immediately for a new company that took the name Reo—having given his name to one company, Olds explained, he had only his initials to give to the next.

By this time the influx into the automobile business was assuming the proportions of a torrent. There are records of over 1500 individuals and firms that have built over 3000 makes of car in the United States, and the great majority of these came and went in the period between the Duryea achievement of 1893 and the First World War. Most of these ventures produced one or two cars and then disappeared, but in what we might call the second wave of American automobile pioneers there were some names that became securely established in automotive history.

Among the builders of gasoline cars was Henry A. Knox, a mechanic of Springfield, Massachusetts, who began to experiment with air-cooled engines in 1897 and put the Knox car on the market three years later, just ahead of the Franklin Manufacturing Company of Syracuse, New York, which started production of the best known early American air-cooled gasoline car in 1902, using a design originally worked out by an engineer named John Wilkinson in 1897. In Buffalo, New York, two bicycle makers turned to automobiles at the turn of the century: George N. Pierce, originally a manufacturer of bird cages and refrigerators, began to build the car that eventually became one of the outstanding luxury vehicles, the Pierce-Arrow; Erwin R. Thomas switched from motorcycles to cars, and the "Thomas Flyer" became famous as the winner of a New York to Paris race (across the United

States and Russia) in 1908. A very famous American automobile was first made in Warren, Ohio, in 1899 by James Ward Packard, engineer and manufacturer of electrical equipment. The story seems well founded that Packard, who had some previous interest in automobiles, bought the twelfth Winton to be built, and when he complained about defects was told by Winton to go and build a better car himself. Packard launched the enterprise, but soon afterward it was taken over by Henry B. Joy, son of the railroad magnate James F. Joy, and moved to Detroit. Henry Joy was an automobile enthusiast; he was also an advocate of highway improvement and was one of the promoters of the Lincoln Highway, the first transcontinental route.

Winton had competition in his own city of Cleveland from F. B. Stearns, a product of the Case School of Applied Sciences, and Paul Gaeth, a skilled mechanic. Both went into business in 1898. Gaeth, very much a perfectionist, made a total of 300 cars by skilled handicraft methods in the twelve years he was in business. Also in Cleveland was Peerless, a company that moved from building washing machines to bicycles to automobiles, reaching the last in 1900. To complete the record, when Peerless had to discontinue the manufacture of cars in 1931, it became a brewery.

Others who must be included in this list are Howard C. Marmon, one of the most brilliant of American automotive engineers, whose family firm in Indianapolis added cars in 1903 to its existing product line of flour-milling machinery; George P. Dorris, who began to build automobiles in St. Louis in 1898; Louis S. Clarke, who started in Pittsburgh in the same year with what later became the Autocar, noteworthy as one of the first American designs to have a shaft drive instead of a chain drive; and Thomas B. Jeffery, whose Rambler bicycle had been the principal competitor of Pope's Columbia and who turned to Rambler cars in Kenosha, Wisconsin, in 1900. The Studebaker Brothers Manufacturing Company of South Bend, Indiana, has to be included also. Its entry into automobile manufacturing was a corporate rather than an individual matter, and the company's commitment to the new operation took place in stages from 1898 to 1904.

The Olds Motor Works left Detroit shortly after the fire to return to Lansing, but there was still ample automotive activity in Detroit. Jonathan D. Maxwell, who had worked as a mechanic for Haynes-Apperson and Olds, left Olds to develop his own car, as did Robert C. Hupp and two University of Michigan products who wished to work in partnership, Roy D. Chapin and Howard E. Coffin. Chapin was the executive and salesman, Coffin the engineer. As an employee of Olds, Chapin distinguished himself by driving a curved-dash Oldsmobile from Detroit to the Automobile Show in New York in 1901. The trip took seven days; he virtually rebuilt the car en route, and in upstate New York he found the towpath of the Erie Canal better than any of the roads. Another Detroiter, David Dunbar Buick, sold a prosperous plumbing supply business in 1899 in order to pursue his ideas about automobile design. He and his associates came up with an excellent technical concept in the valve-in-head engine, but they were unable to get into production; Buick died in poverty while his car became the nucleus of General Motors.

During this time Henry Ford found financial support to go into automobile manufacturing, but while Ford acquired a reputation as a racing driver, he was likewise unable to get into production. His backers replaced him with Henry M. Leland, who was head of the machine tool firm of Leland and Faulconer and had previously had experience making engines for Olds. In Leland's hands the organization was transformed into the Cadillac Motor Car Company. Leland was a precisionist who left his mark on the American automobile industry by insisting on rigorous standards of accuracy. Later on he would leave Cadillac and found Lincoln when he was almost eighty years old.

All these men were primarily interested in gasoline automobiles, yet it was by no means certain when the twentieth century arrived that the motor vehicle of the future would have an internal combustion engine.

Steam and electricity were still active competitors. Thomas A. Edison clearly identified the limitations of the electric automobile as early as 1896, but for local travel it still had advantages over the noisy and clumsy gasoline engines of the day—not the least being that a woman could operate an electric automobile easily while a gasoline car required the onerous and dangerous task of cranking.

The most spectacular American venture into electric automobiles was the previously mentioned Electric Vehicle Company. It was a promotion by a group of New York financiers for a plan to operate electric cabs in major American cities. They took over the Morris and Salom firm and subsequently added Pope's motor carriage division to do their manufacturing. The electric cabs were a failure; they had to carry batteries weighing a ton, which had to be recharged after every trip. The Electric Vehicle Company went into receivership; its place in automotive history is not its own product, but the fact that it came into control of the Selden patent.

Others had a more modest and practical approach. One was Andrew L. Riker, an ex-law student from Columbia who built an electric tricycle in 1884 and organized a company to build electric automobiles in 1898. He sold out to the Electric Vehicle Company after little more than a year of independent operation. Others of note were the Woods Motor Vehicle Company of Chicago, which also went into business in 1898 and operated cabs with some success, and Waverley Electric of Indianapolis, which made electric automobiles from 1896 to 1915. For some years Waverley was part of the Pope organization, for Pope, after selling its first motor vehicle business to the Electric Vehicle Company, decided that this had been a mistake and returned to the automobile field. From 1901 to 1907, when Pope went into receivership, Waverley was Pope-Waverley, along with a line of gasoline cars: Pope-Hartford, Pope-Toledo, and Pope-Tribune. Another electric car to appear in 1898 was the Baker, the creation of Walter C. Baker of Cleveland, a graduate of Case. Seven years later the Rauch and Lang Carriage Company of Cleveland also began to make electrics, and the two merged in 1915 as Baker and Raulang. When the market for electric automobiles vanished, Baker and Raulang survived as manufacturers of electric industrial trucks.

The steam automobile had, and still has, its ardent partisans. The most famous American steamer was the Stanley, designed by Francis E. and Freelan O. Stanley, twin brothers from Lewiston, Maine, who had previously been engaged in ventures as remote from the horseless carriage as making violins and photographic plates. In 1896 they acquired the rights to a steam car designed by George D. Whitney of Providence, Rhode Island, and began manufacturing a year later. Then they sold their business to a syndicate from which two companies were formed: Mobile, in Tarrytown, New York; and Locomobile, in Bridgeport, Connecticut. The former was short-lived, but Locomobile had a long career as a luxury car—not, however, as an electric. It converted to gasoline in 1902, interestingly enough with Riker as chief engineer. The Stanleys resumed operations on their own in 1901. Francis died in an automobile accident in 1918 and Freelan then lost interest.

The steam automobile had some distinct advantages. It had great power—a Stanley was the first car to climb Mount Washington (1899), and a Mobile went all the way up Pikes Peak in 1900; and, as with the electric, there were no gears to shift. On the other hand, the first models required at least twenty minutes to get up steam, and the boiler capacity was good for only about forty miles. These deficiencies were remedied in the White steamer, which appeared in 1901. It was designed in Cleveland, Ohio, by the three sons of Thomas H. White, founder of the White Sewing Machine Company; the White Motor Company, indeed, built its first cars in the sewing machine factory. The White had a flash boiler, initially introduced in France by Léon Serpollet in 1889, which gave steam in two minutes, and a condensing system that permitted 200 miles of running on one filling of the boiler. These features were adopted by the Stanleys and others, but they were not enough to preserve the steam automobile. People were afraid of the high-pressure boilers (600 psi), although there is no record of any disastrous boiler explosion on a steam car. But maintenance was expensive, and once the gasoline engine was sufficiently refined, the steam car was doomed. The Whites, like the Locomobile Company, saw what was coming and turned to gasoline automobiles in 1909. They made an equally fortunate decision a few years later, when during World War I they gave up the manufacture of passenger cars to concentrate on commercial vehicles.

The horseless carriage era may be considered to have ended in 1903, the date of the founding of the Ford Motor Company. After that the story of the American automobile became one of the growth of large-scale business enterprise, of the development of production techniques with far-reaching economic consequences, and of a widespread use of motor vehicles that brought major changes in American society. The beginning of this transformation occurred approximately in the decade preceding World War I. Four aspects may be singled out.

First, the vehicle itself ceased to be a horseless carriage and became recognizably an automobile, following the basic design already established by E. C. Levassor in France and F. W. Lanchester in Great Britain. The buggy pattern disappeared. The engine was put in front, where its weight helped to hold the vehicle on the road. Four- and six-cylinder engines replaced the old "one-lungers"; an eight-cylinder engine was tested in 1907, and the V-8 appeared on high-priced cars in 1915. The tillers used on the early cars were superseded by steering wheels, especially after the introduction of an efficient steering knuckle in 1902. The most important single American contribution during this period to the technology of the car itself was the electric starter, developed by the Cadillac Motor Car Company and Charles F. Kettering and introduced in 1912. It can be credited with insuring the final triumph of the internal combustion engine as the source of power for motor vehicles by eliminating the most serious drawback the gasoline car had—that is, the need to start it by cranking.

Second, the automobile industry was freed from having its growth impeded by patent difficulties. When the Electric Vehicle Company attempted to enforce the Selden patent claims, it had to accept a licensing arrangement administered by a body known as the Association of Licensed Automobile Manufacturers (A.L.A.M.), which hoped to use the patent to stabilize the industry. Henry Ford, however, challenged the A.L.A.M. after being refused a license and in a long, historic lawsuit won his case. The validity of the Selden patent was upheld, but only for vehicles using the two-cycle, constant-pressure Brayton engine which had been Selden's original inspiration. The automobile industry then adopted an agreement for the cross-licensing of patents, to avoid such suits in the future.

Third, the process began whereby automobile manufacturing would come to be concentrated in a few very large companies. The Ford Motor Company was one of these almost from its inception, but Ford is a special case to be discussed separately. The origin of General Motors can be traced back to 1904, when the faltering Buick operation was taken over by William C. Durant, son of a wealthy family in Flint, Michigan, an aggressive promoter and salesman, and at the time a very successful carriage manufacturer. Durant put Buick on its feet and then developed a plan for a great combination making several types of car and controlling its own sources of parts and components. After one or two false starts he incorporated General Motors in 1908, built around four major passenger car manufacturers (Buick, Cadillac, Oldsmobile, Oakland) and a host of lesser firms. He expanded too ambitiously, ran into financial troubles in 1910, and temporarily lost control of General Motors to a bankers' syndicate. He then joined forces with a former Buick racing driver named Louis Chevrolet to manufacture a low-priced car with Chevrolet's name. Its success enabled Durant to recover his position in General Motors in 1915, again temporarily. During the interim General Motors had been run by James H. Storrow, a blue-blood Boston banker, and Charles W. Nash, a onetime migrant farm laborer who had risen to be head of the Durant-Dort Carriage Company and later of Buick. To take Nash's place at Buick, they brought in Walter P. Chrysler, born a Kansas farm boy and trained as a locomotive mechanic.

Durant's principal rival in trying to effect a great automotive combination was Benjamin Briscoe, who, with his brother Frank, had been a successful sheet metal manufacturer in Detroit. The Briscoes tried to help David Buick, but they gave up and joined with Jonathan D. Maxwell under the name of Maxwell-Briscoe. Benjamin Briscoe was briefly associated with Durant's first efforts at combination. Later, in 1910, he organized the United States Motor Company, but he too got over-extended and the combination became insolvent in 1912. It was reorganized, without Briscoe, as the Maxwell Motor Car Company, and became the ancestor of the Chrysler Corporation.

A third promoter-salesman, John N. Willys, had a more promising start. He sold bicycles and later automobiles in Elmira, New York, until in 1907 he took control of a small automobile firm in Indianapolis named Overland—this because Willys concluded that the only way to get deliveries of cars he had ordered was to manage the company himself. Overland was moved to Toledo and became for many years a popular low-priced car. Willys gradually built an automotive empire which showed considerable promise until it was hurt by the short but severe panic of 1920.

There were others which seemed equally likely to achieve dominating positions in the automobile industry. Studebaker absorbed some lesser companies and was a full-fledged automotive power by 1910. The race was wide open. It was easy to get into automobile manufacturing. All that was needed in plant and equipment were some tools and a place to assemble the car. The enterprise could finance itself by buying parts from suppliers on credit and selling the finished product to dealers for cash. In practice, however, only the well managed and adequately financed firms could survive the fierce competition—as, for example, Hudson, founded in 1908 by Roy D. Chapin and Howard E. Coffin, who represented a unique combination of administrative and technical skill. The company and the car were named for J. L. Hudson, the Detroit department store magnate, who provided the initial capital.

Fourth, and most important of all, the American automobile industry gave to the world the first completely integrated and coordinated system of mass production. This achievement centers on Henry Ford and his desire to produce a "car for the great multitude." He was not the only man, and perhaps not even the first, to see the possibilities of a low-priced car for a mass market. Olds, for instance, made a definite effort in this direction. Ford and his associates succeeded because, instead of concentrating on designing a car that could be built cheaply, they first designed a car to meet the requirements of the market and then turned their attention to the problem of producing it in quantity at low unit cost.

The Model T Ford—the "flivver," "Tin Lizzie"—was sturdy and simple, intended for easy and economical operation and maintenance. Its chassis stood high off the ground because the car was meant to be used where roads were poor, even nonexistent. Introduced in 1908, the car was immediately popular, because of both its outstanding serviceability and its down-to-earth ungainliness, which over the years made it the butt of innumerable jokes. The next step was to mass-produce the Model T, and this was achieved by the moving assembly line, tried first for magnetos in 1908 and gradually extended until complete assembly-line production of the entire car was begun at the Ford Motor Company plant at Highland Park, Detroit, on January 1, 1914—the same day that Henry Ford startled the world by announcing a basic wage rate of five dollars a day. The measure of the achievement can be seen in the fact that for almost ten years the Ford Motor Company made half the motor vehicles in the entire world.

Ford's assembly-line revolution coincides closely enough with the reorganization of General Motors so that the two together constitute a decisive phase in the history of the American automobile. The formative period was over, and the pattern of the future was rather clearly defined. There is a fascination about this formative period for anyone who has an interest in cars or in the vital contribution of the automobile to American life. The men and the companies of this era are an assorted and fascinating group; so too are the cars themselves. We have them in this volume—a selection of meaningful vehicles illustrated by Clarence Hornung, with illuminating and informative notes on them by James J. Bradley.

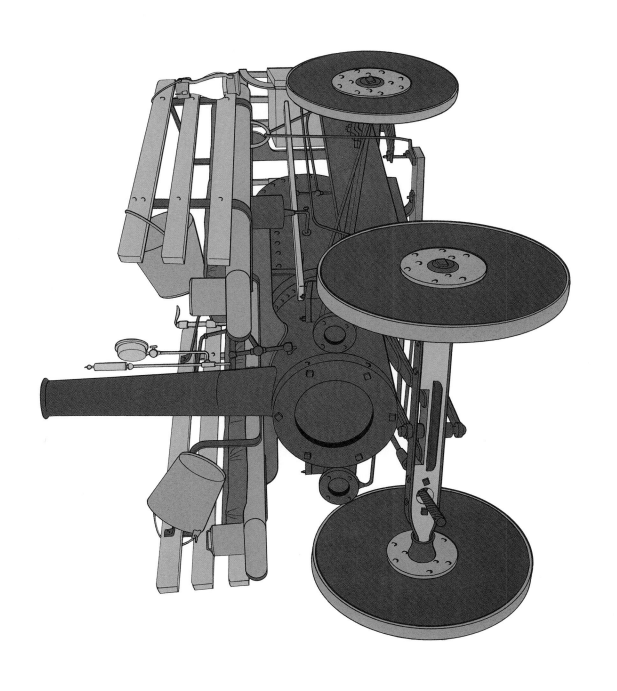

*Dudgeon Steam Wagon    1853*

PLATE 1

Roper Steam Carriage    1863

PLATE 2

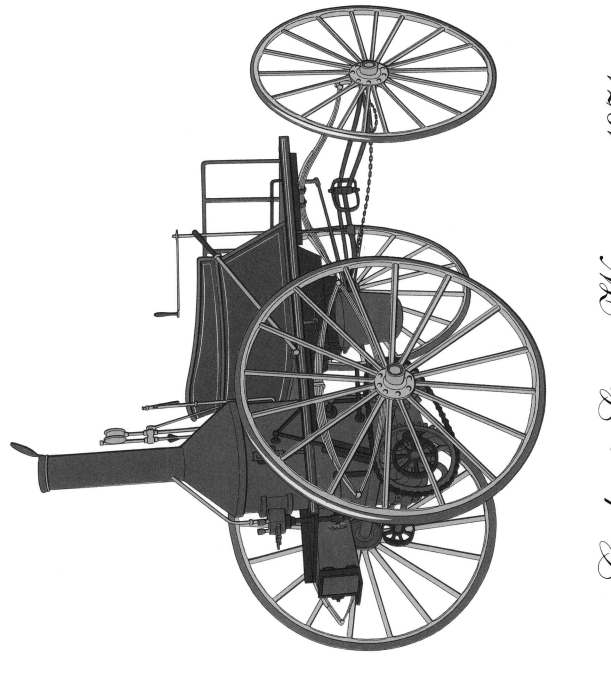

Carhart Steam Wagon     1871

PLATE 3

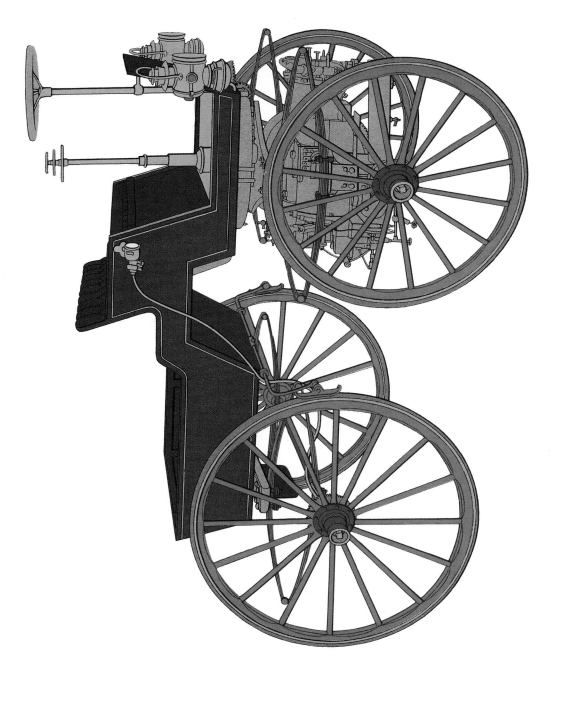

*Selden Road Wagon    1877*

PLATE 4

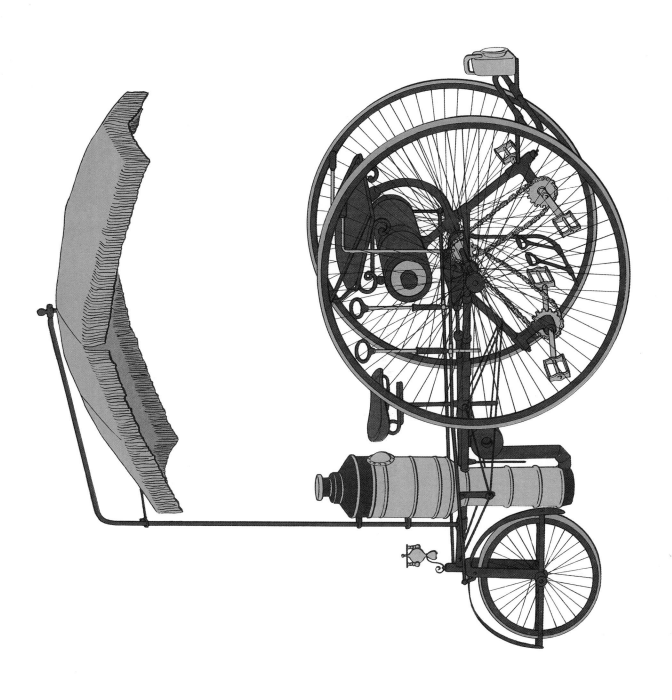

*Copeland Steam Tricycle    1886*

PLATE 5

*Morrison-Sturgis Electric 1890*

PLATE 6

*Nadig Road Wagon 1891*

PLATE 7

Lambert Gasoline Buggy    1891

PLATE 8

*Schloemer–Toepfer Carriage 1892*

PLATE 9

*Duryea Gasoline Buggy*    *1893*

PLATE 10

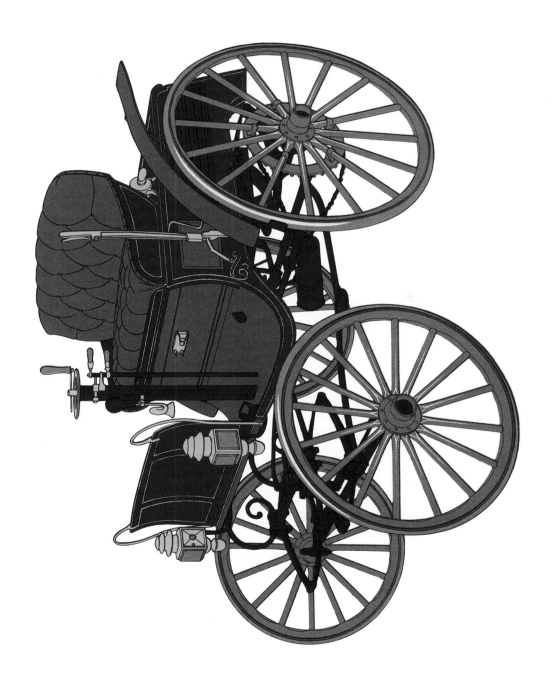

*Black Gasoline Carriage   1893*

PLATE 11

Haynes Gasoline Carriage    1894

PLATE 12

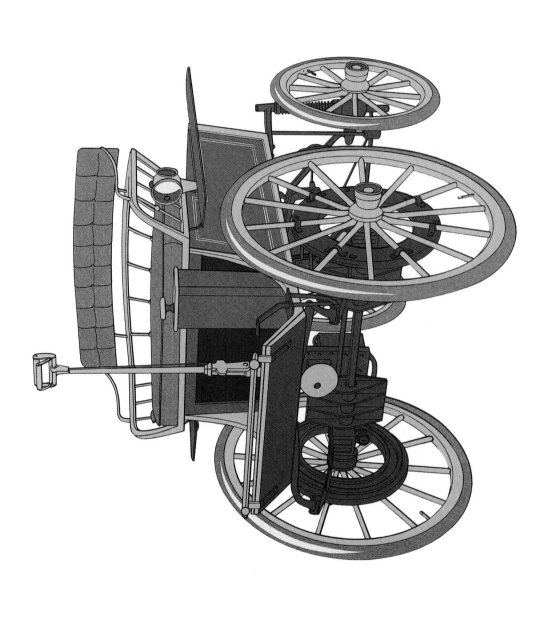

*Morris & Salom Electrobat   1895*

PLATE 13

*Holtzer-Cabot Electric* 1895

PLATE 14

Duryea Motor Wagon    1895

PLATE 15

*Ford Quadricycle    1896*

PLATE 16

King Horseless Carriage 1896

PLATE 17

*Mueller Motor Carriage 1897*

PLATE 18

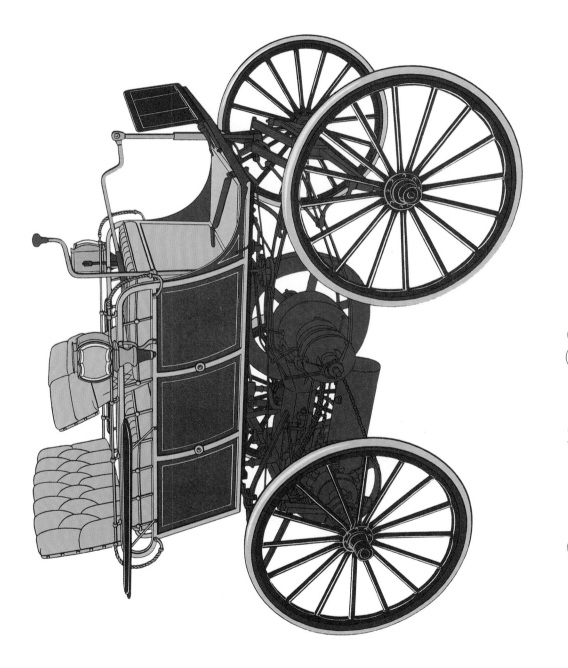

*Olds Motor Carriage     1897*

PLATE 19

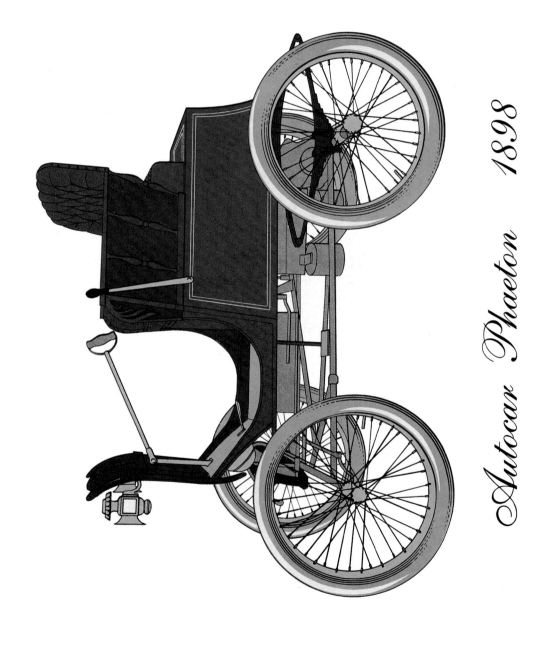

*Autocar Phaeton 1898*

PLATE 20

Woods Electric Hansom 1898

Plate 21

Ford Gasoline Carriage   1898

Plate 22

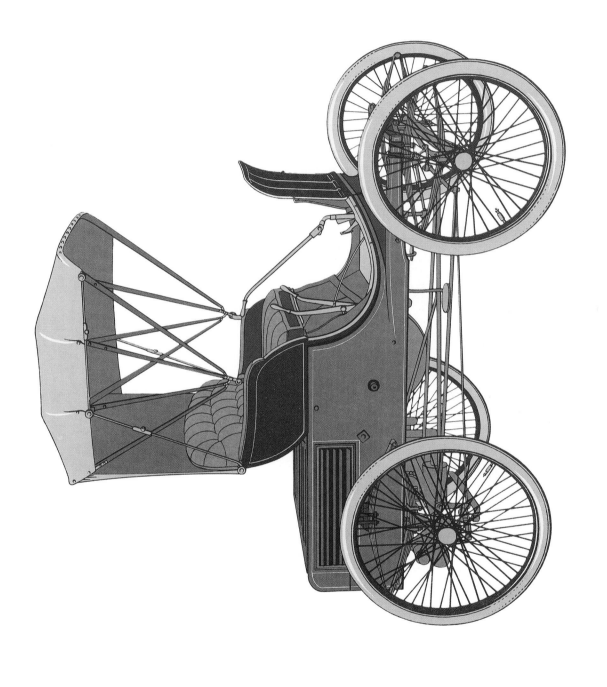

*Winton Motor Carriage    1898*

PLATE 23

*Riker Electric Tricycle    1898*

PLATE 24

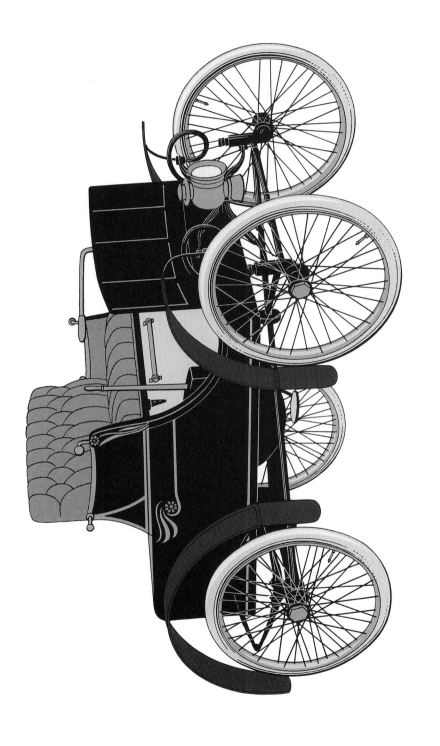

Packard Model "A" 1899

PLATE 25

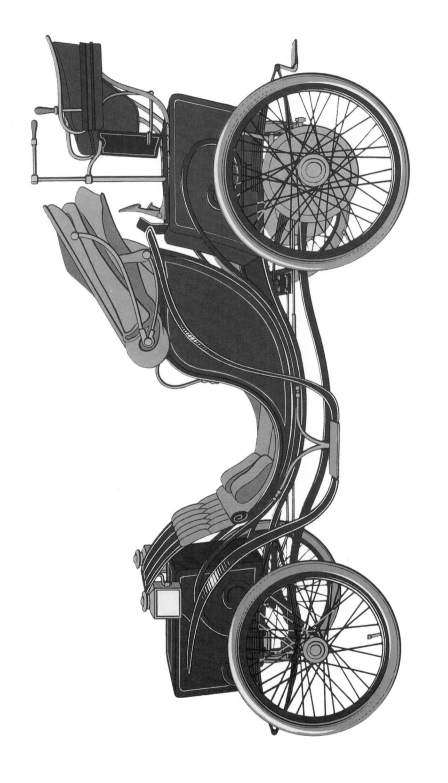

*Columbia Daumon Victoria    1899*

PLATE 26

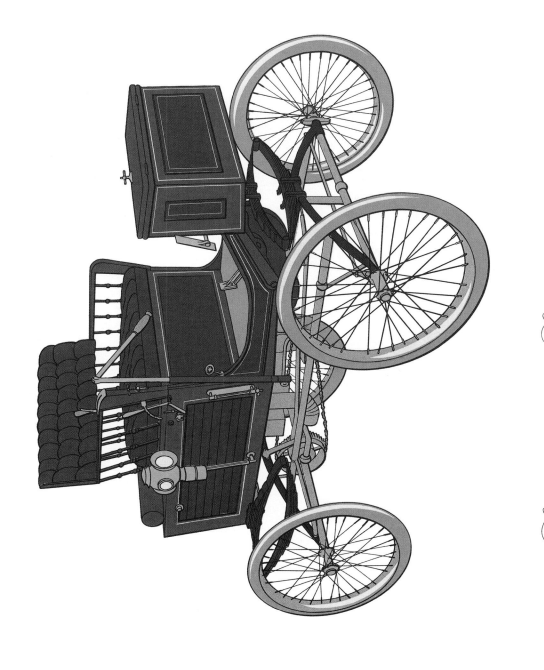

*Locomobile Steamer    1899*

PLATE 27

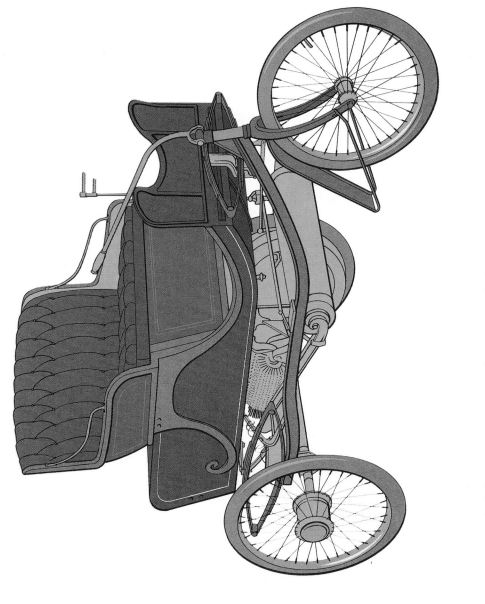

Knox Three-Wheeler  1899

PLATE 28

*Riker Electric Brougham    1900*

PLATE 29

Woods Station Wagon   1900

PLATE 30

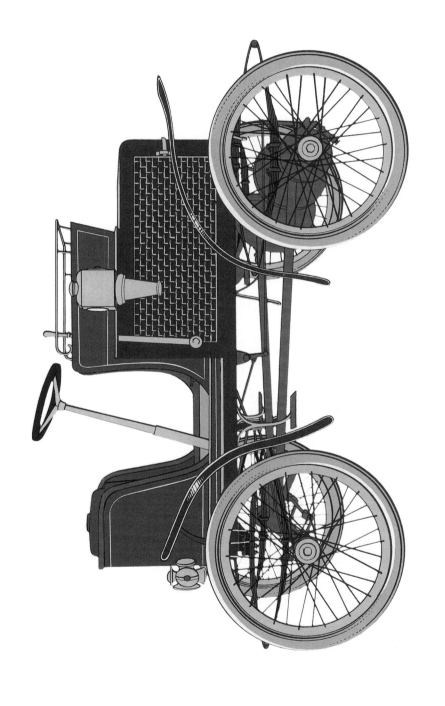

*Columbia Electric Phaeton   1900*

PLATE 31

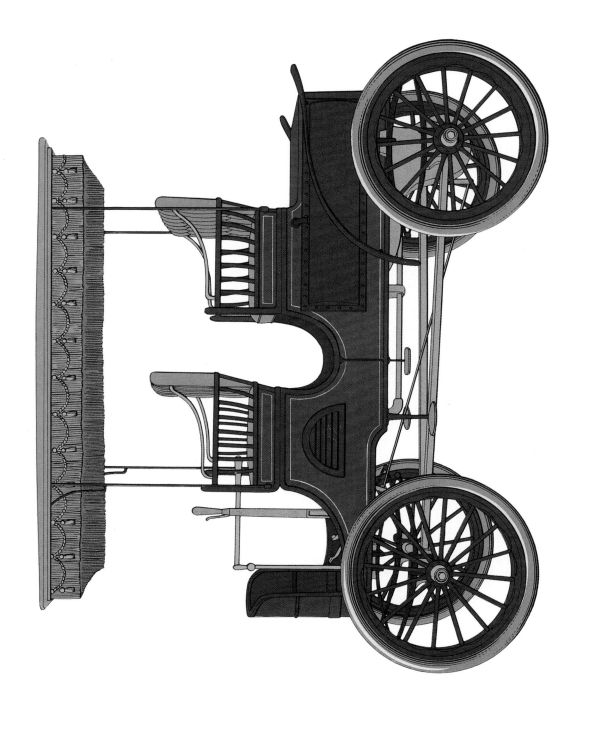

*Haynes–Apperson Surrey   1901*

PLATE 32

Riker Theater Bus    1901

PLATE 33

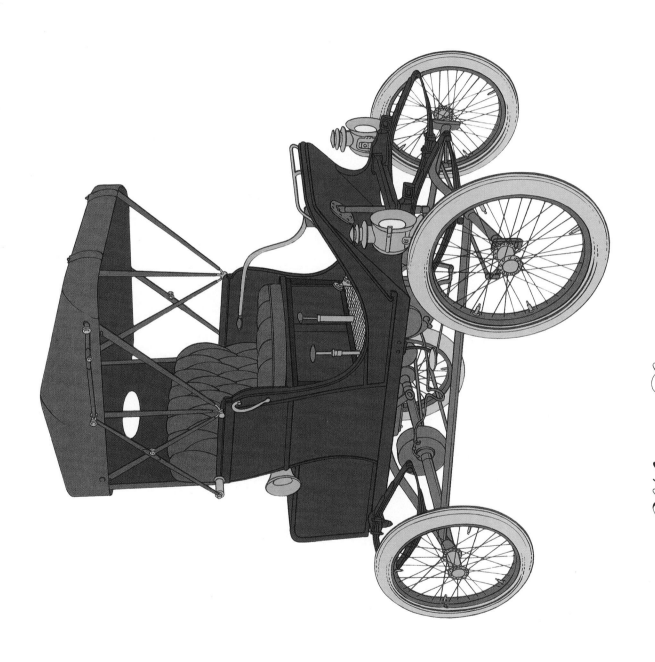

*White Steamer   1901*

PLATE 34

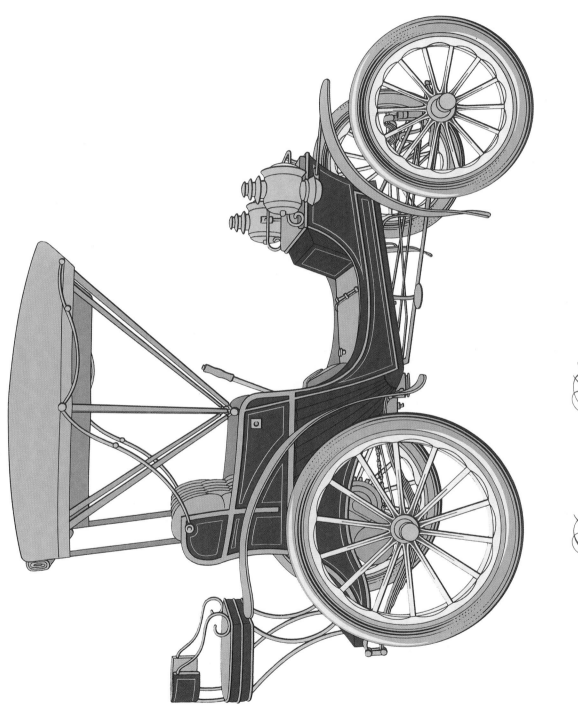

*Duryea Phaeton    1902*

PLATE 35

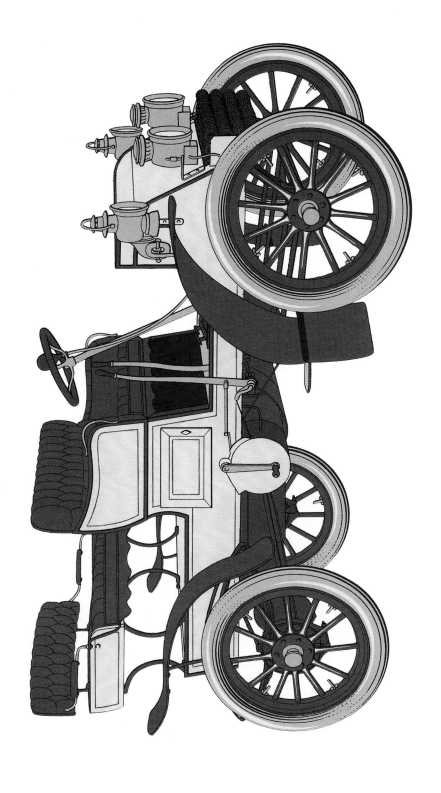

*Packard "F" Tonneau    1902*

PLATE 36

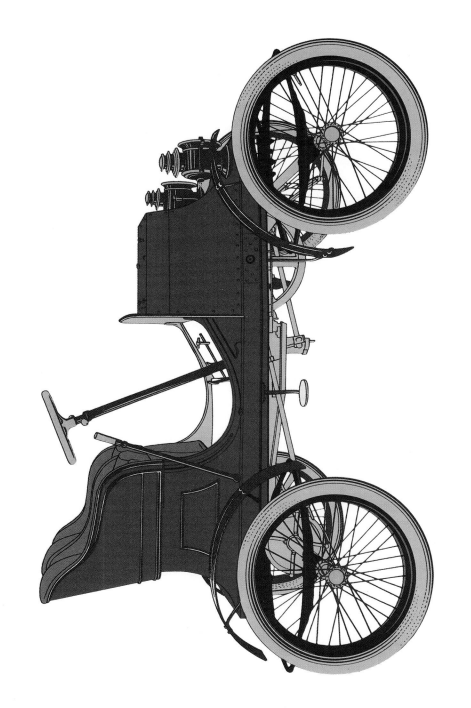

*Franklin Runabout    1902*

PLATE 37

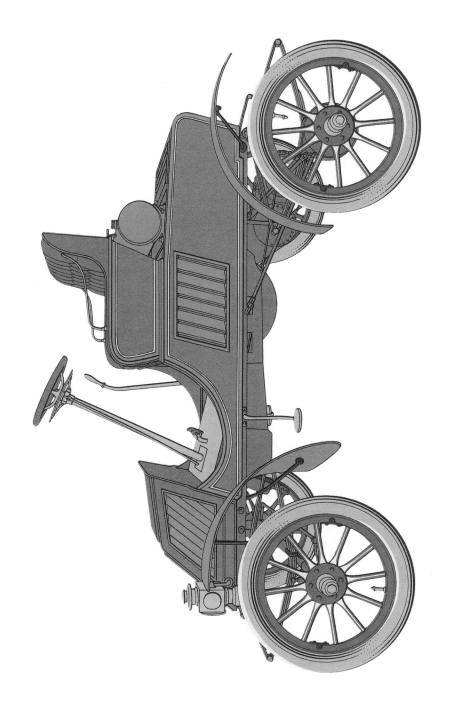

Rambler Runabout 1902

PLATE 38

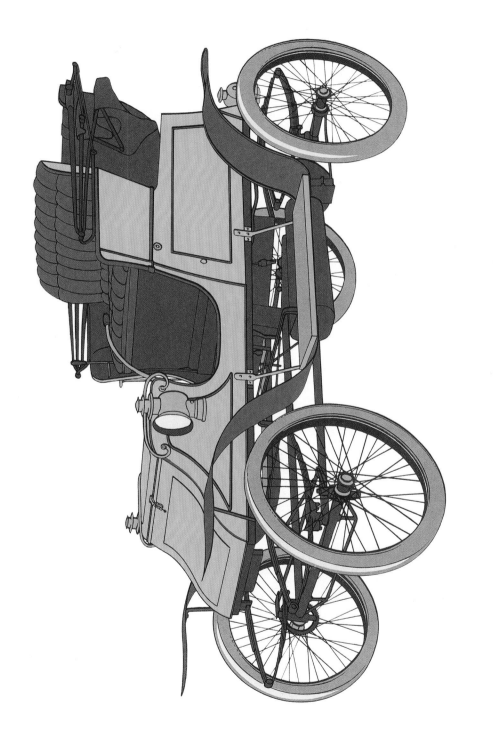

Stanley Steamer   1902

PLATE 39

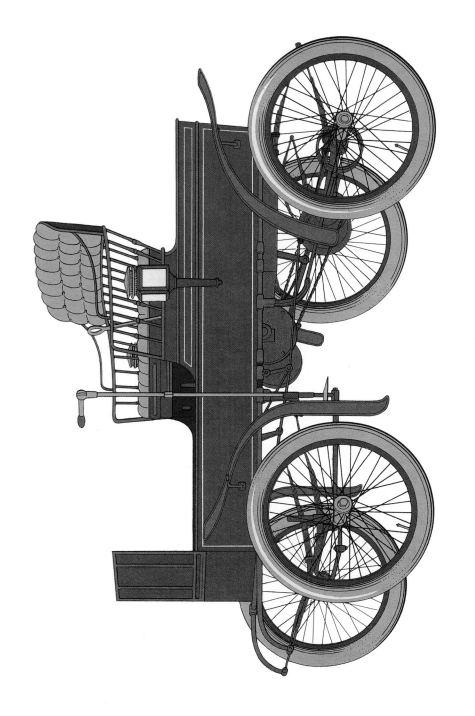

*Studebaker Electric Runabout 1902*

PLATE 40

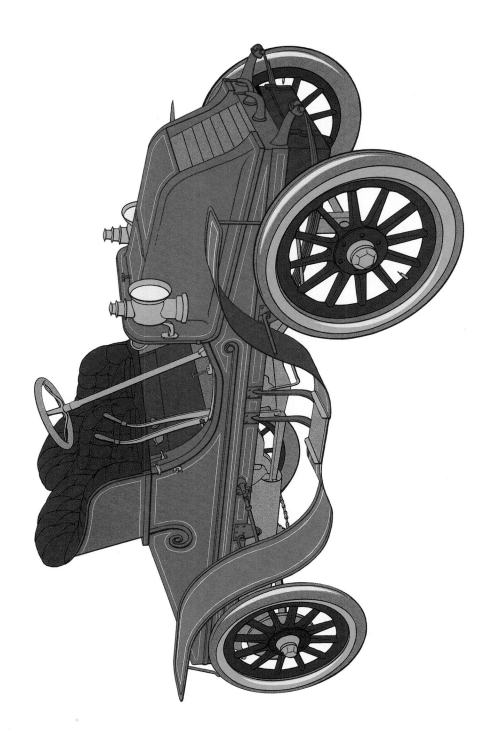

Winton Touring Car    1903

PLATE 41

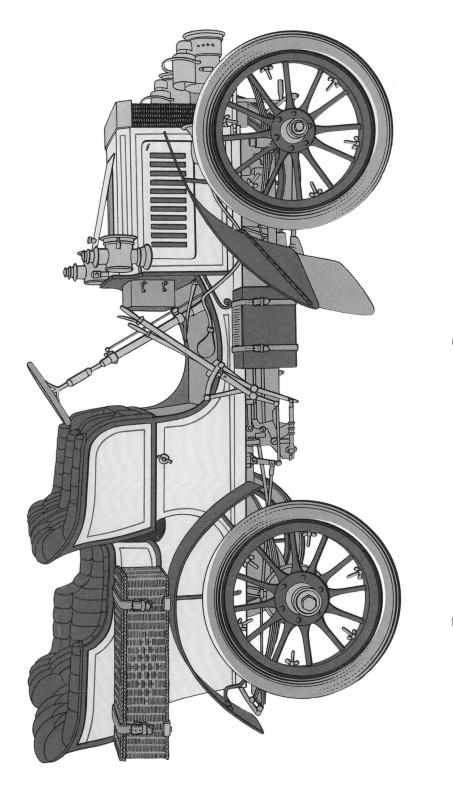

*Peerless Touring Car    1903*

PLATE 42

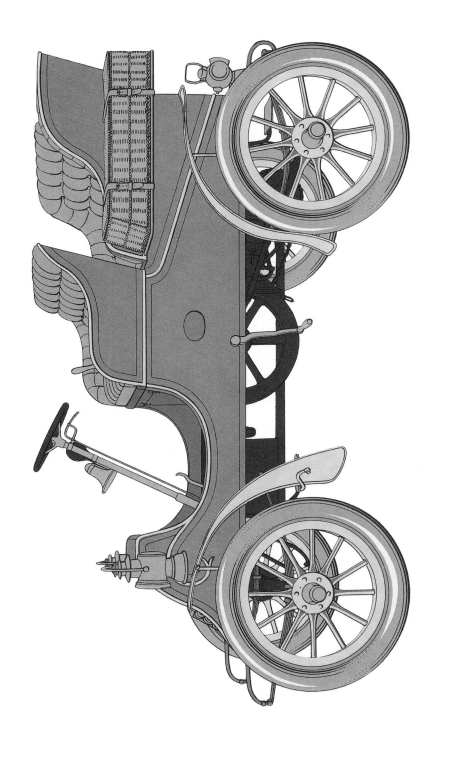

Cadillac Tonneau    1903

PLATE 43

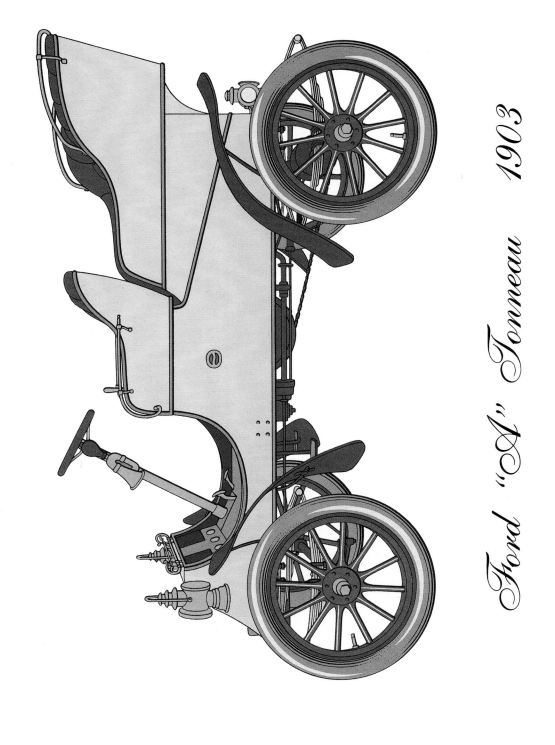

Ford "A" Tonneau    1903

PLATE 44

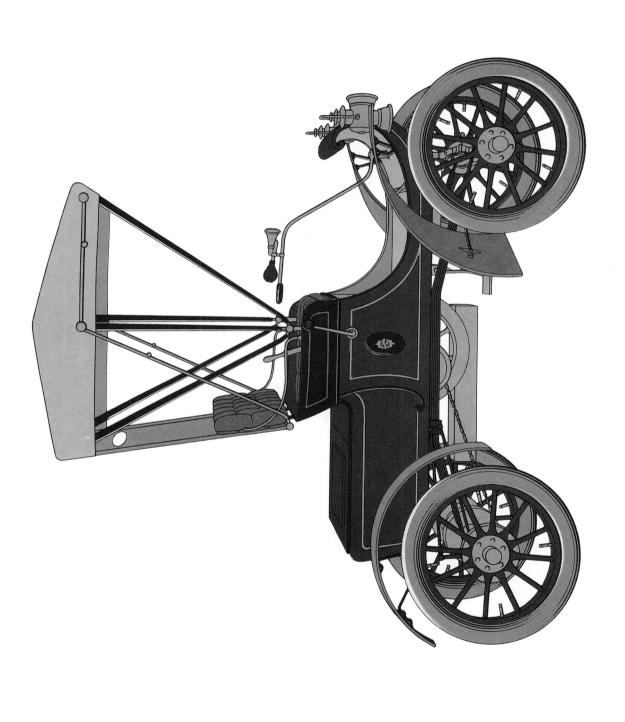

Oldsmobile Curved Dash Runabout   1903

PLATE 45

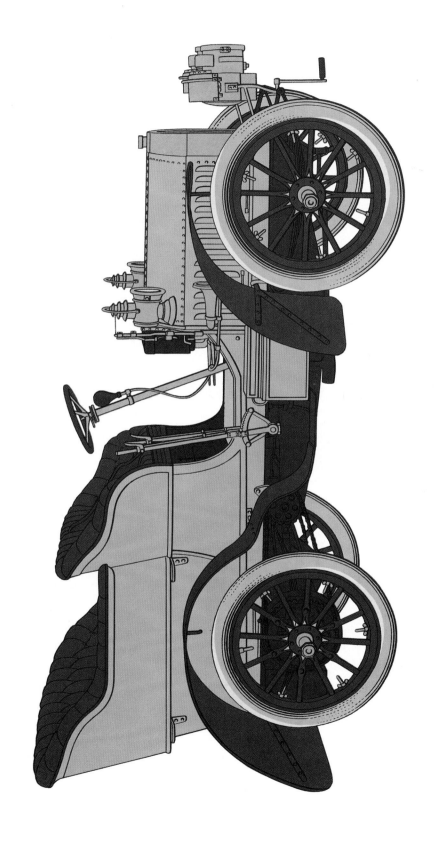

Locomobile Tonneau De Luxe 1904

PLATE 46

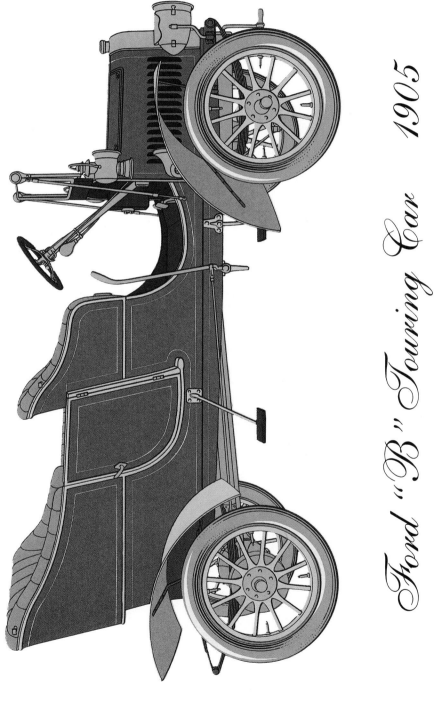

*Ford "B" Touring Car    1905*

PLATE 49

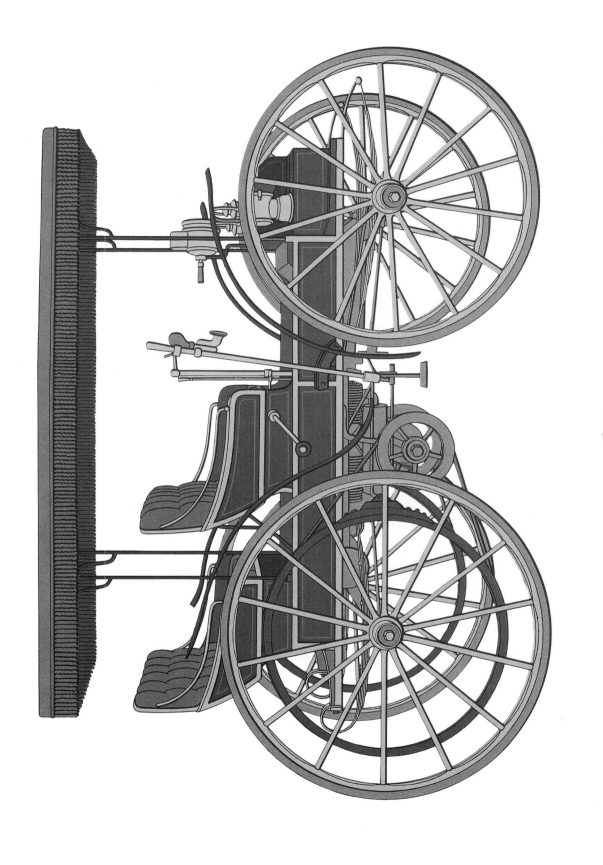

*Holsman Surrey    1905*

PLATE 50

Cadillac "D" Touring Car    1905

PLATE 51

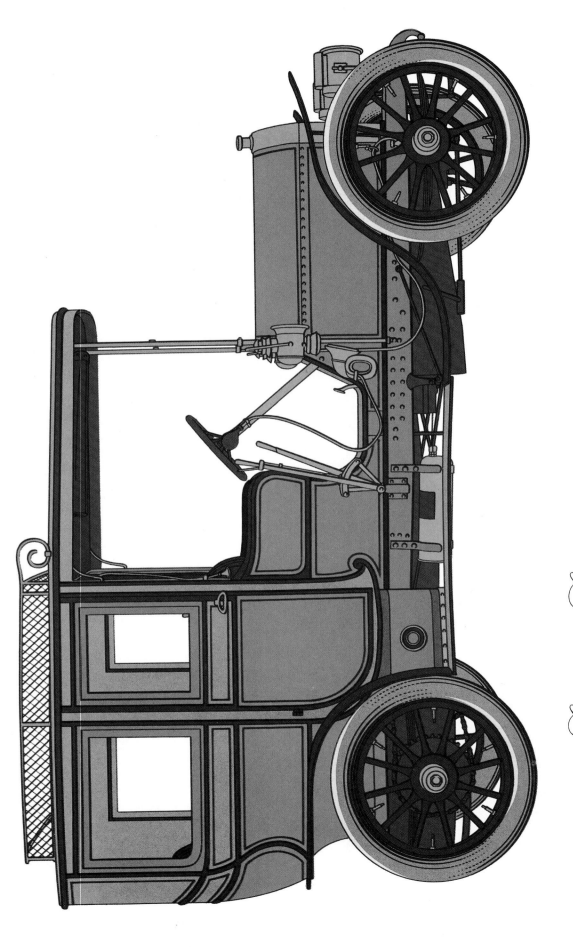

Stearns Limousine "40-45" 1906

PLATE 52

Ford "K" Touring Car 1906

PLATE 53

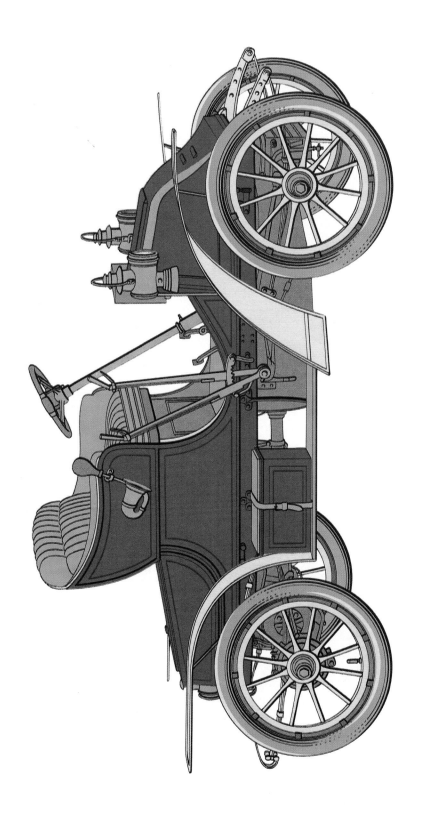

*Autocar Runabout 1906*

PLATE 54

Marmon "D" Touring Car 1906

PLATE 55

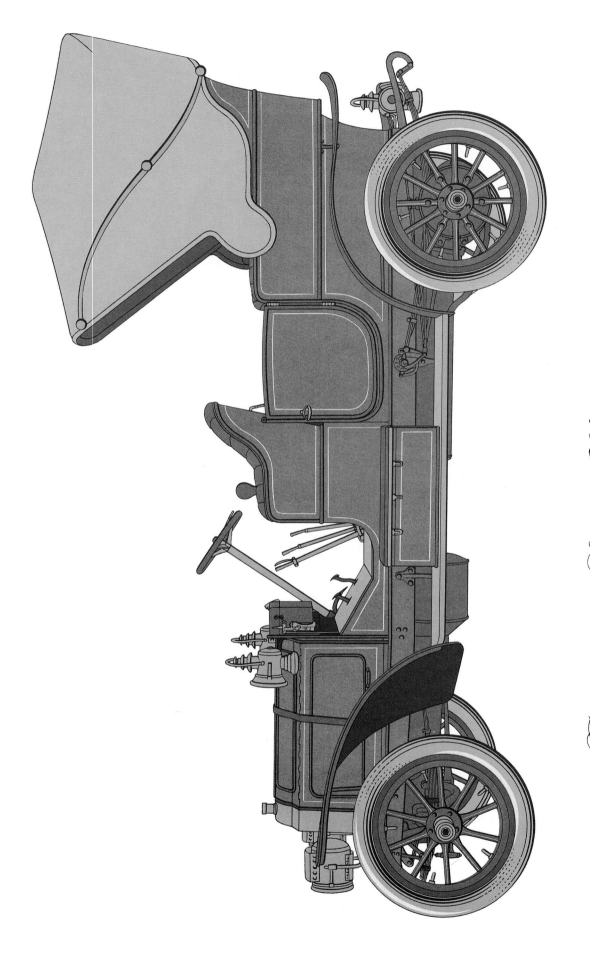

*Packard "S-24" Victoria    1906*

PLATE 56

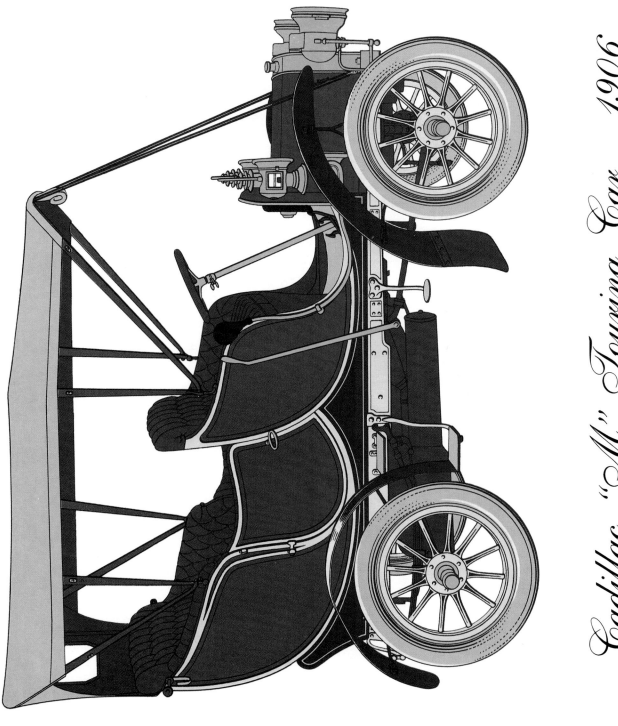

Cadillac "M" Touring Car 1906

PLATE 57

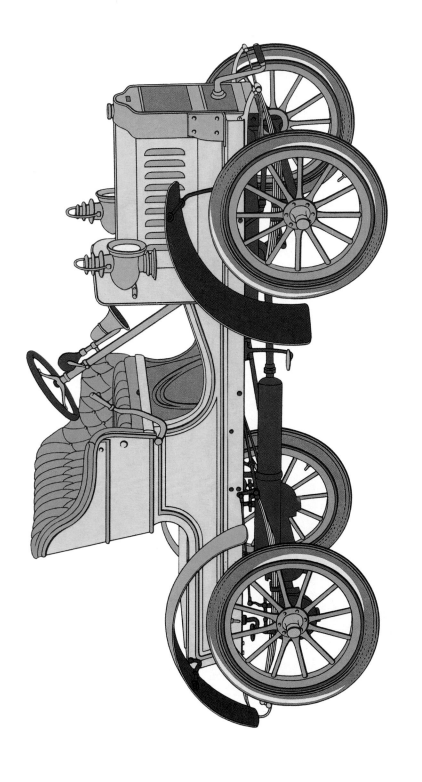

*Maxwell Tourabout   1907*

PLATE 58

Apperson Touring Car    1907

PLATE 59

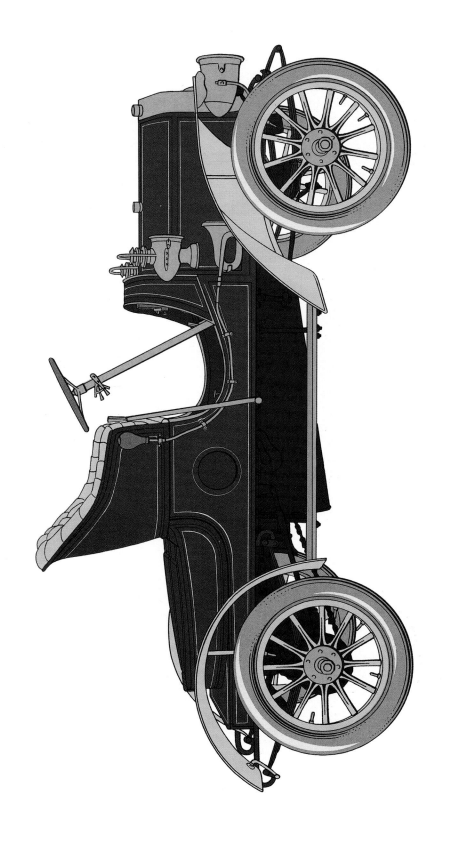

Buick "G" Runabout 1907

PLATE 60

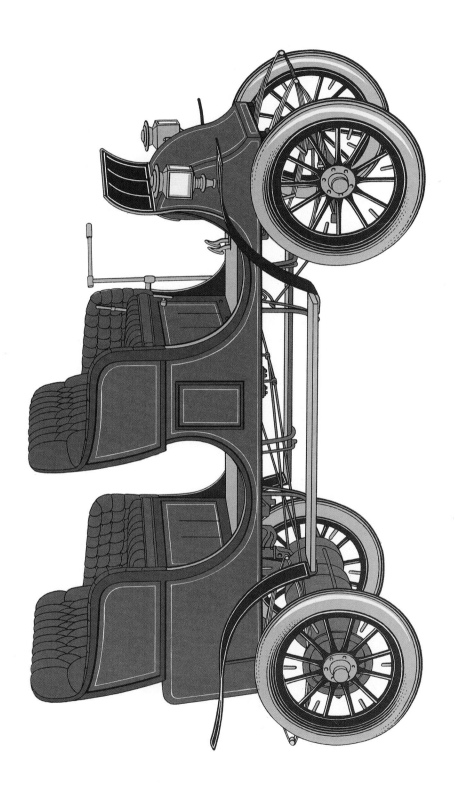

Pope–Waverley "60-A" Surrey    1907

PLATE 61

Cadillac "H" Limousine 1907

PLATE 62

Oldsmobile "A" Touring Car   1907

PLATE 63

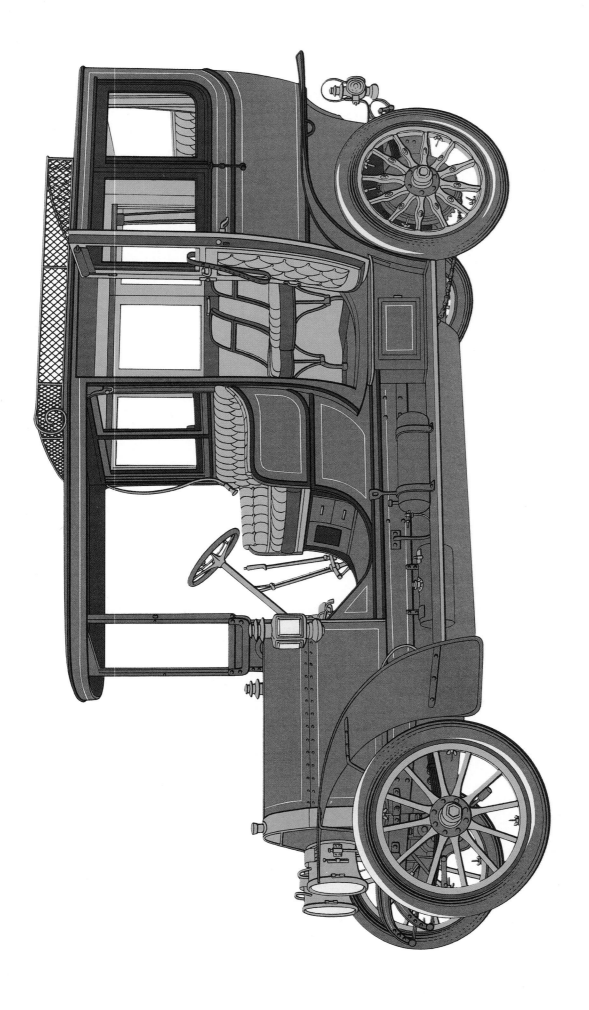

S. & M. Simplex Limousine   1907

PLATE 64

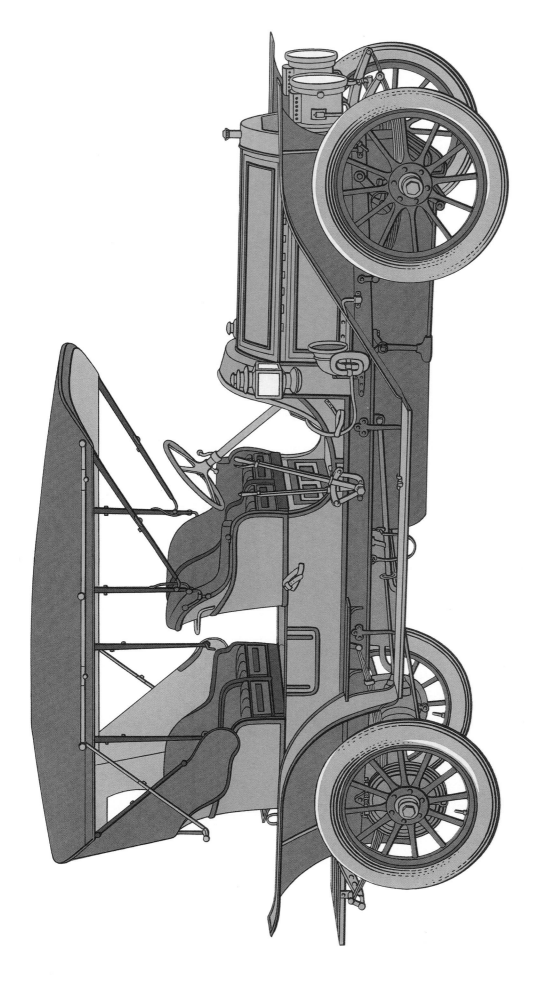

Pierce Great Arrow Touring Car   1908

PLATE 65

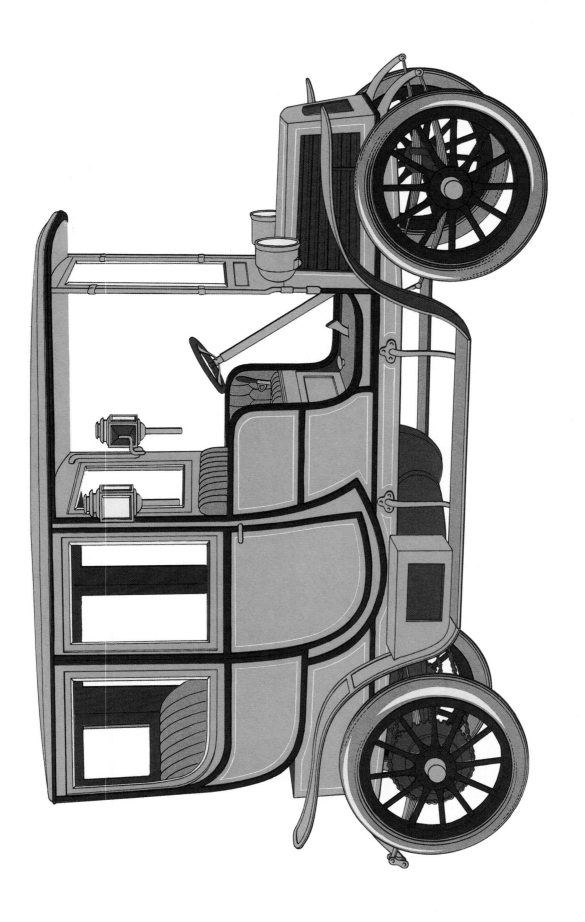

*Rauch & Lang Brougham   1908*

PLATE 66

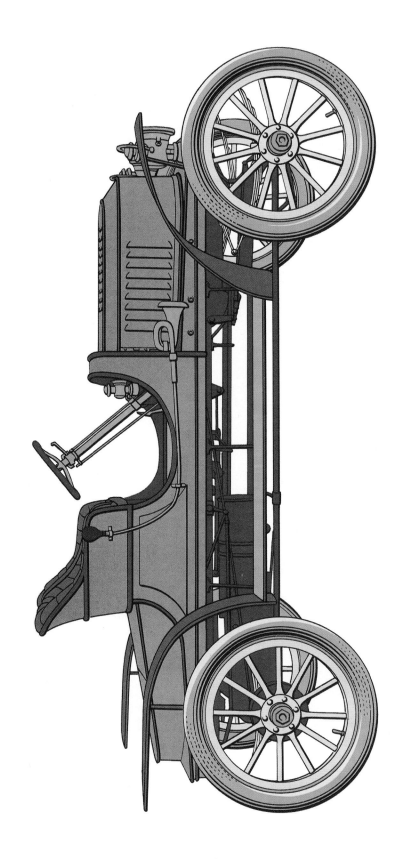

*Stanley Roadster 1908*

PLATE 67

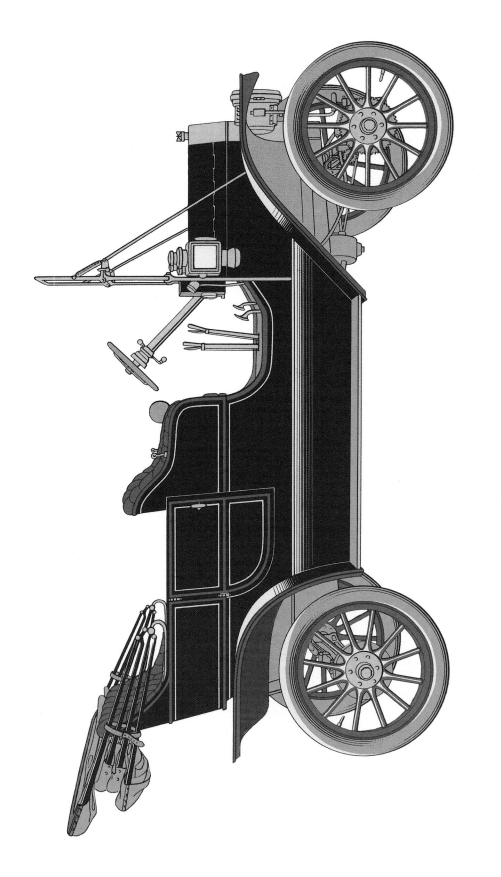

Ford Model "T" Touring Car    1909

PLATE 68

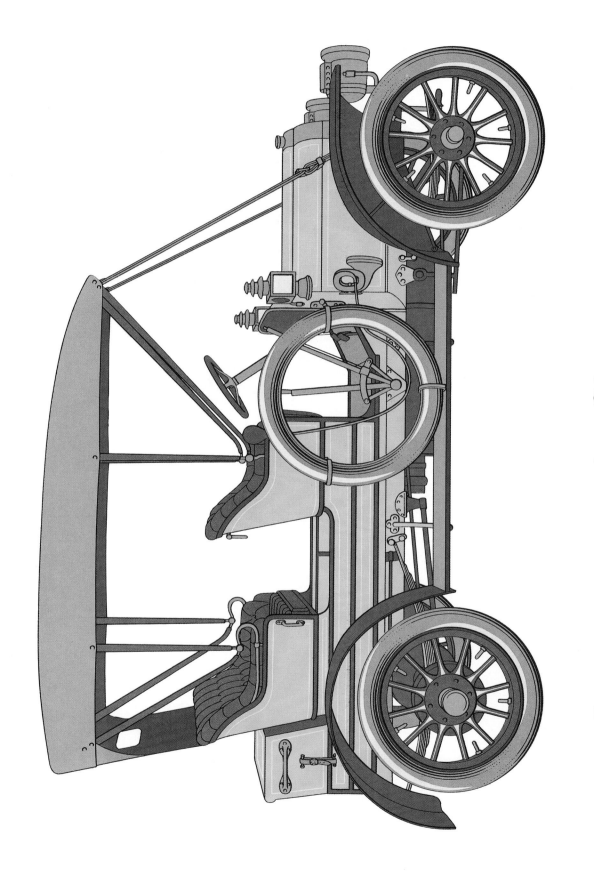

Studebaker "A" Suburban 1909

PLATE 69

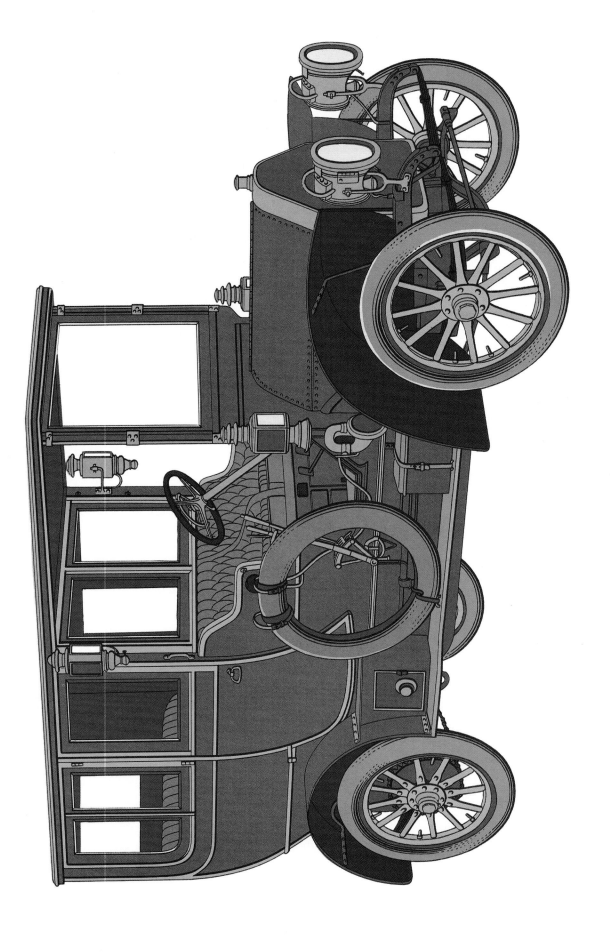

*Knox "M" Limousine    1909*

Plate 70

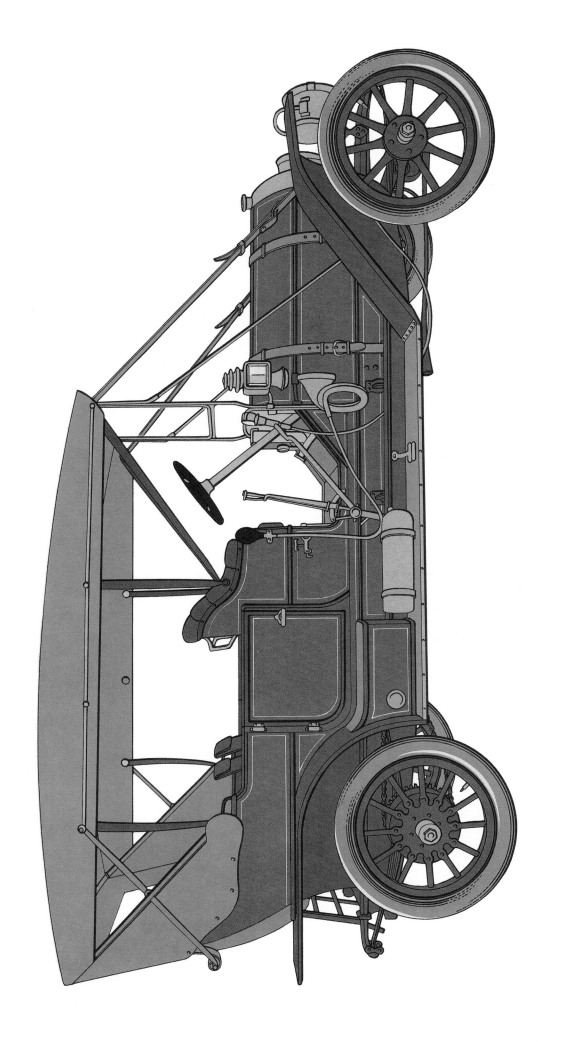

Thomas Flyer Touring Car    1909

PLATE 71

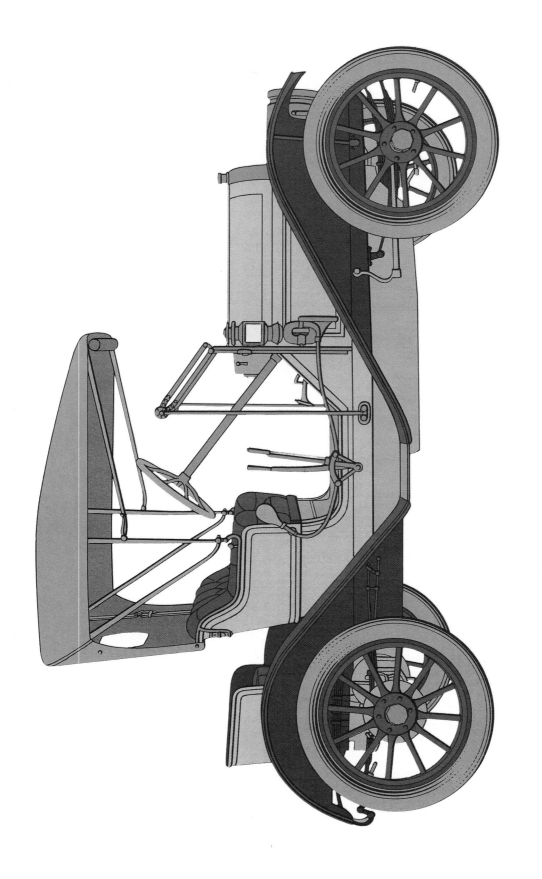

Hudson Roadster 1910

PLATE 72

*Chalmers-Detroit Coupé    1910*

PLATE 73

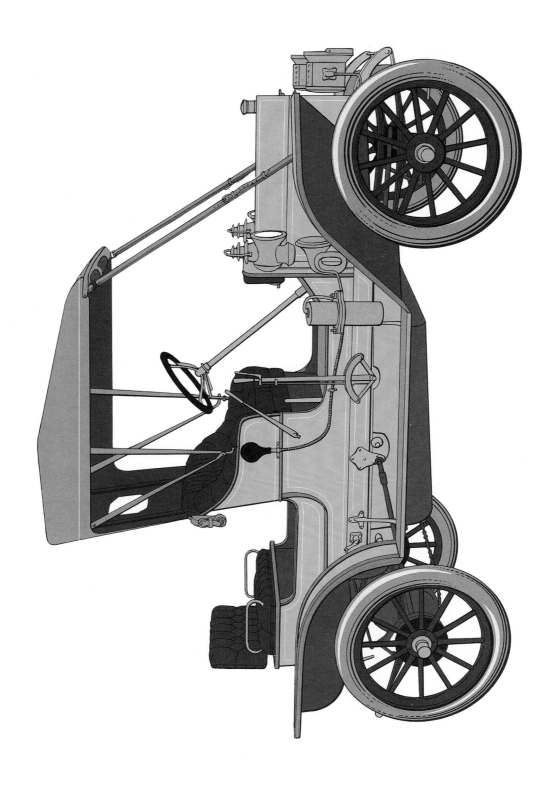

Reo Roadster    1910

PLATE 74

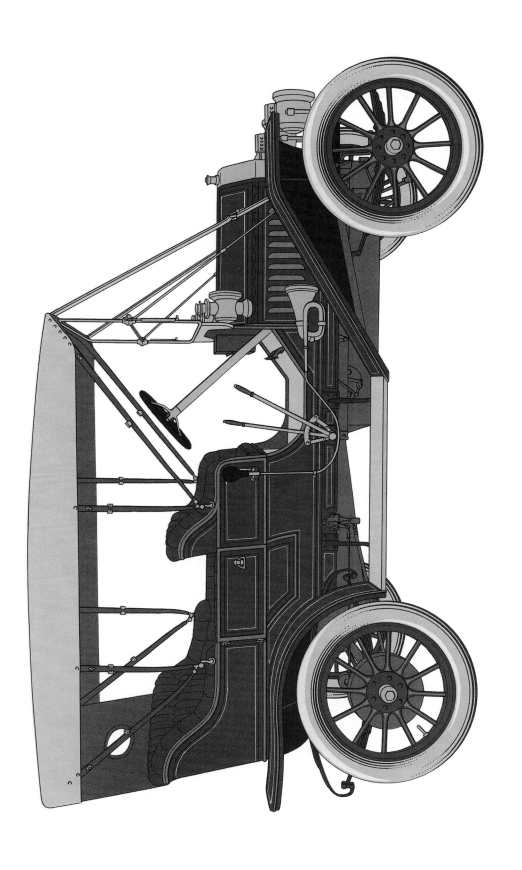

Buick "10" Toy Tonneau   1910

PLATE 75

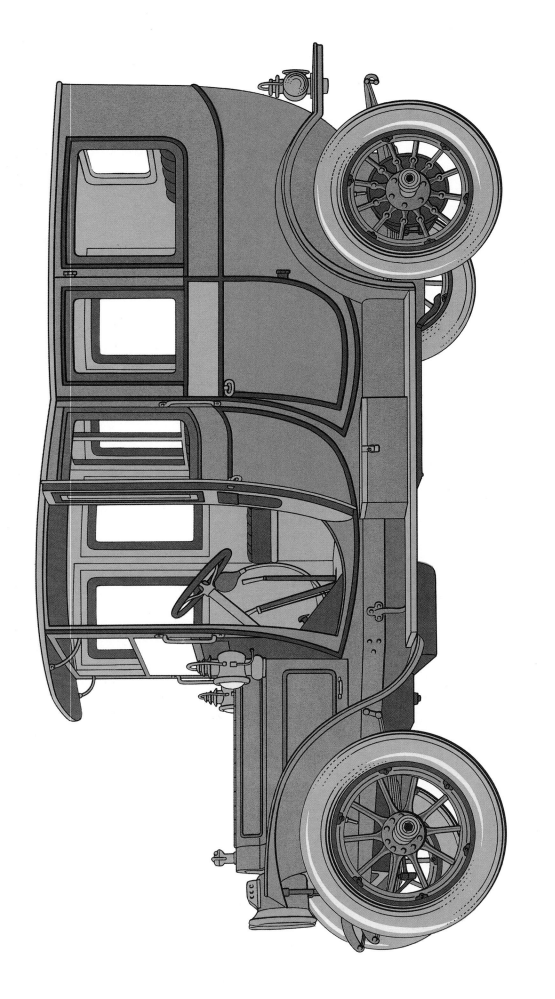

*Packard Berline   1910*

PLATE 76

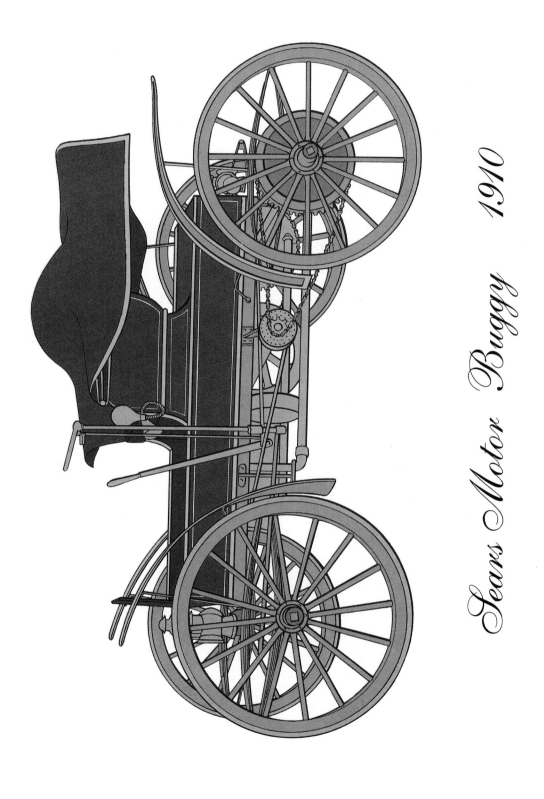

Sears Motor Buggy  1910

Plate 77

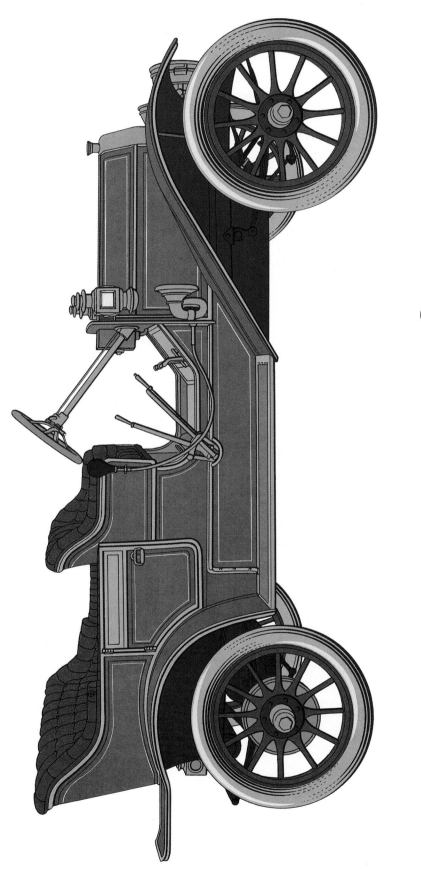

Oakland "K" Touring Car   1910

PLATE 78

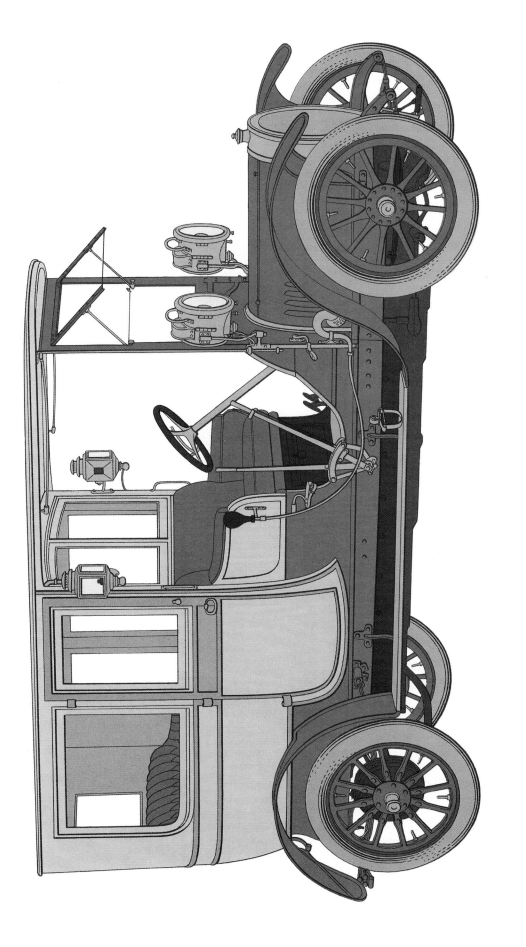

*Brewster Limousine  1911*

PLATE 79

Alco Touring Car   1911

PLATE 80

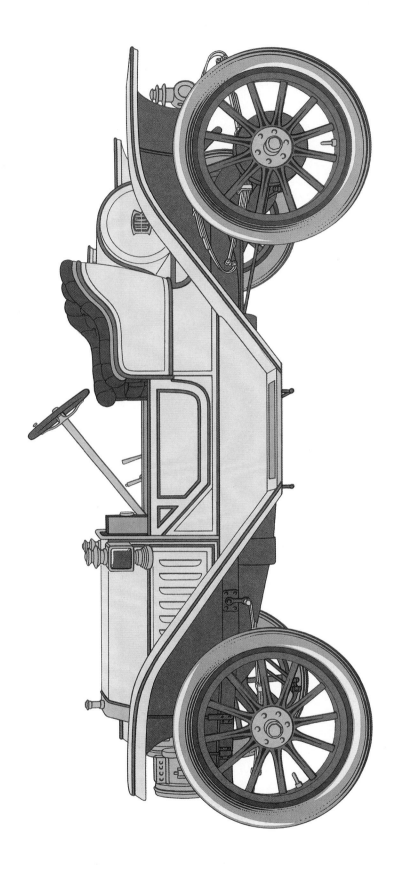

Buick "26" Runabout   1911

PLATE 81

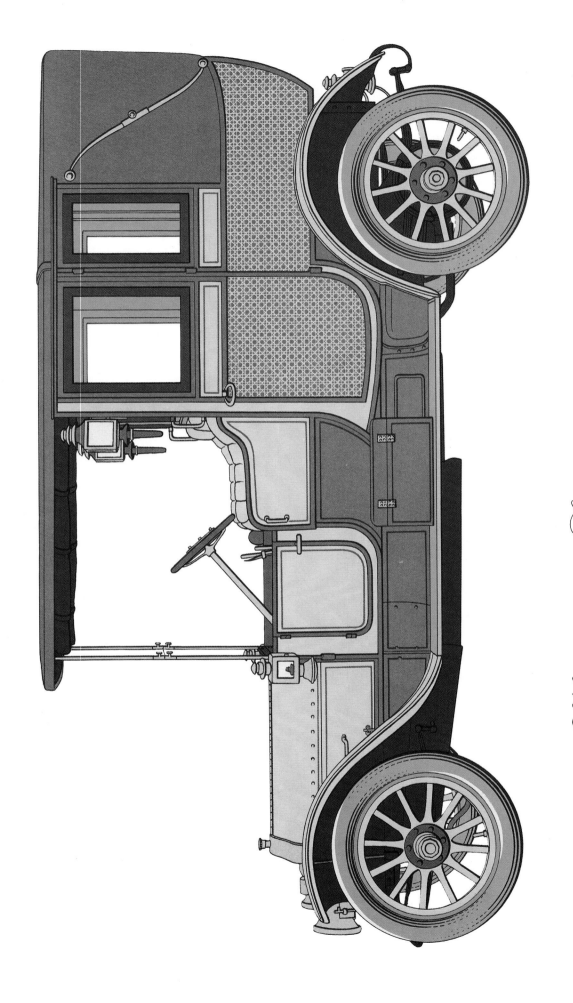

*White "30" Landaulet   1911*

PLATE 82

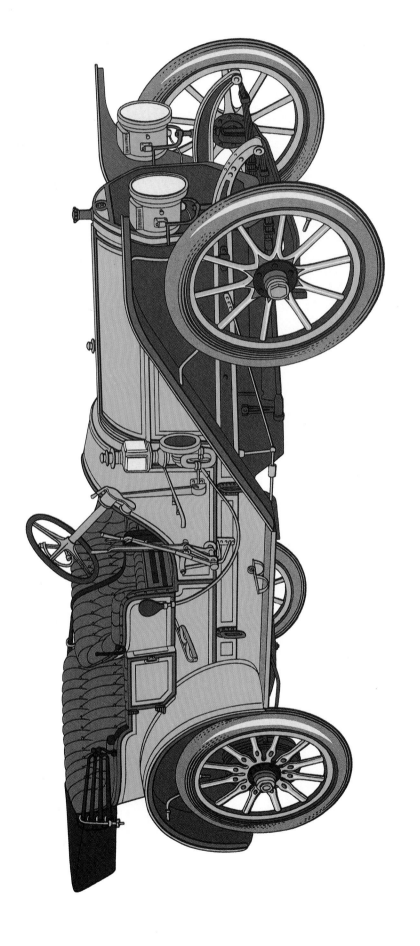

Matheson Joy Tonneau   1911

PLATE 83

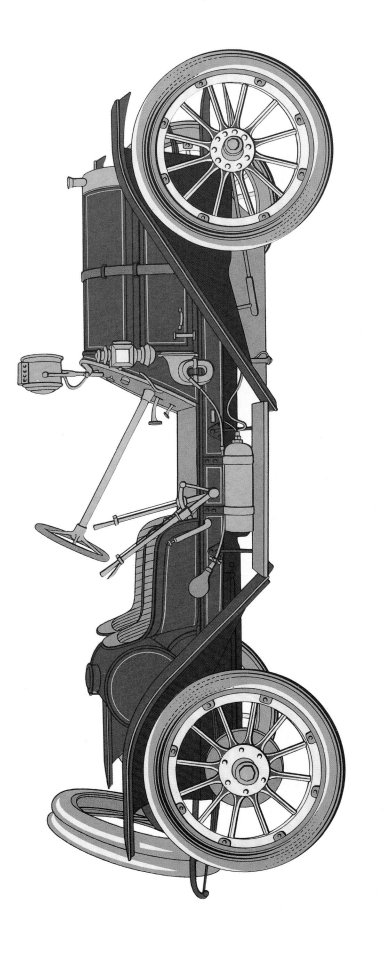

Mercer Raceabout    1911

PLATE 84

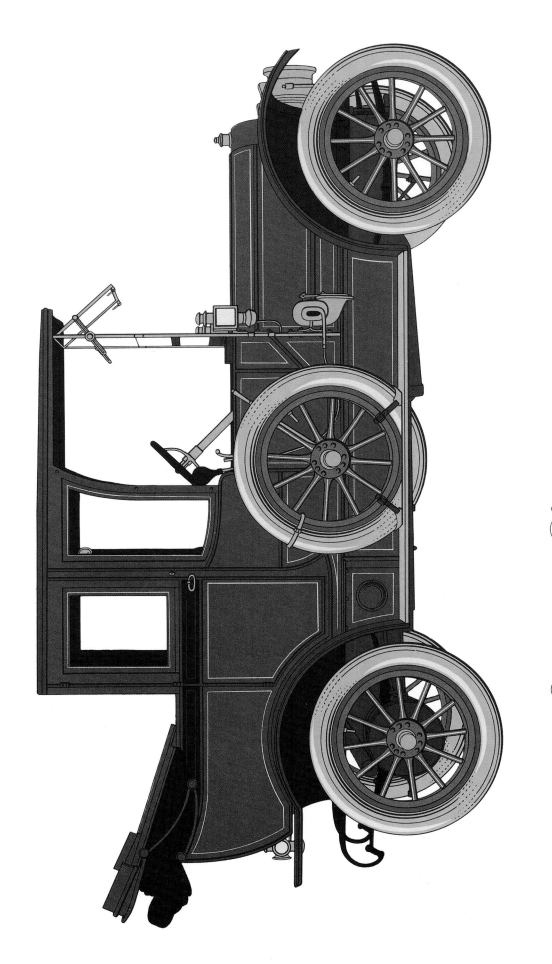

*Rambler Landaulet 1911*

PLATE 85

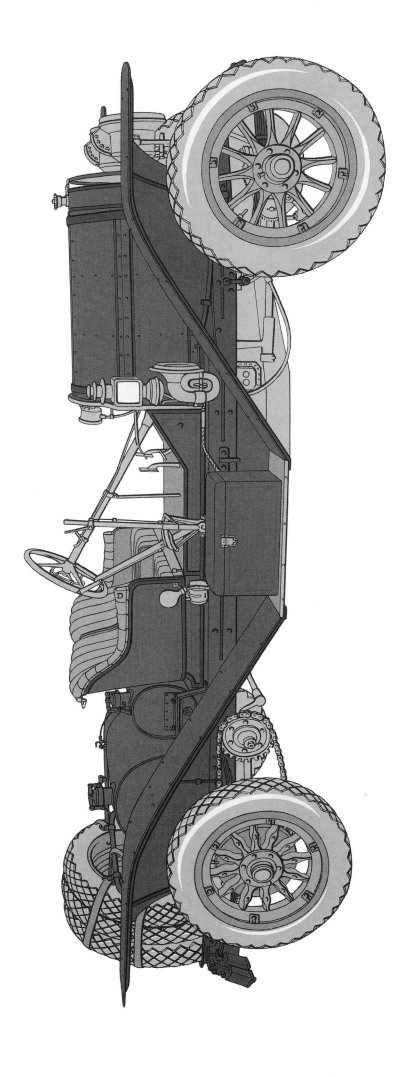

Simplex Speedster 1912

PLATE 86

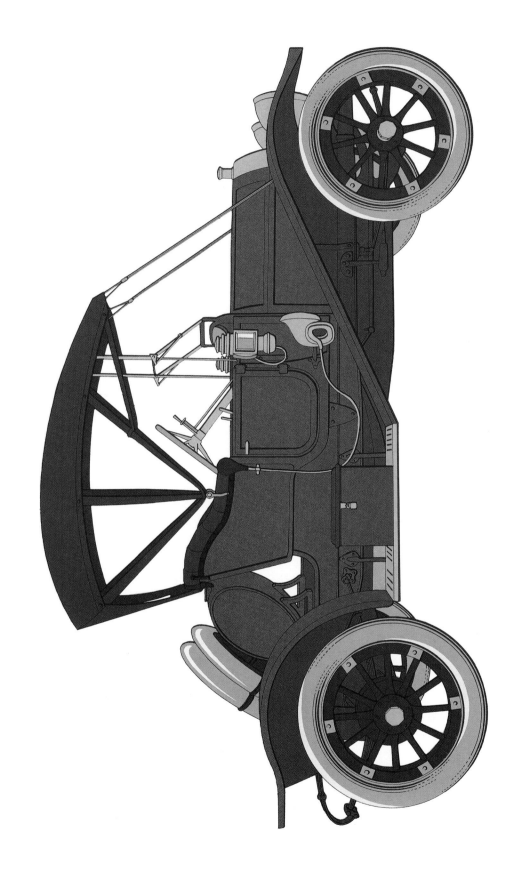

*Abbott–Detroit "30" Roadster    1912*

PLATE 87

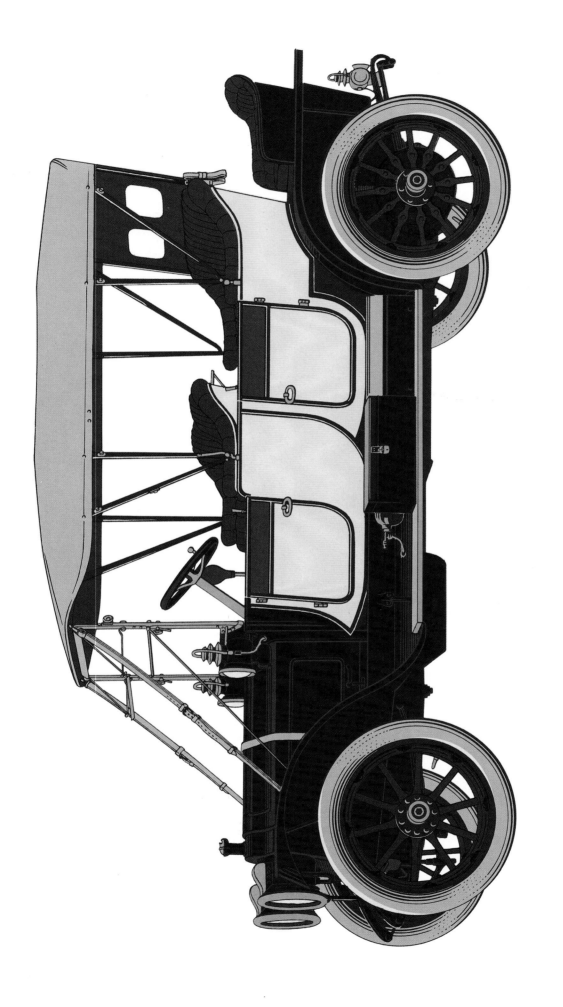

Packard "30" Close-Coupled    1912

PLATE 88

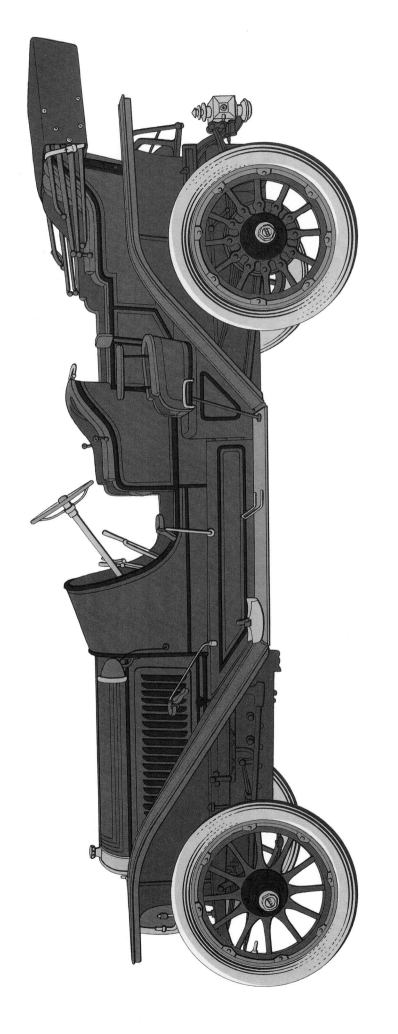

*Lozier Toy Tonneau   1912*

PLATE 89

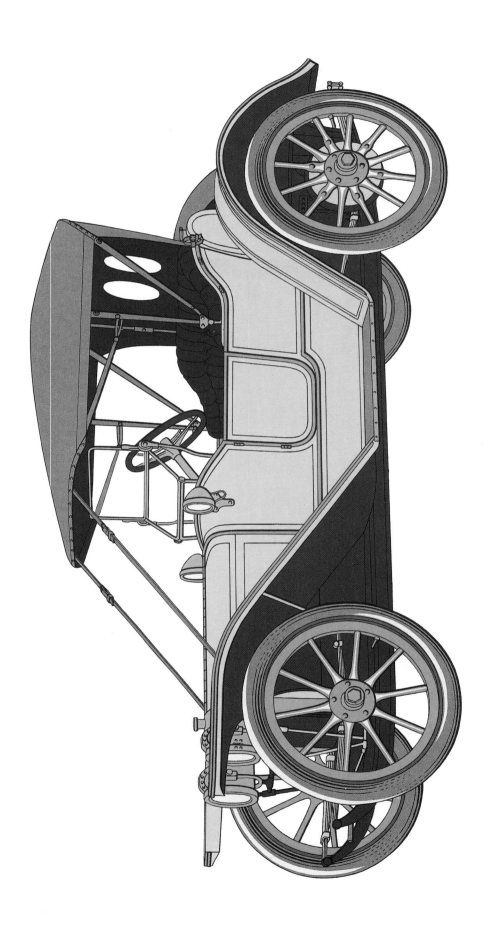

American "22-B" Roadster 1913

PLATE 90

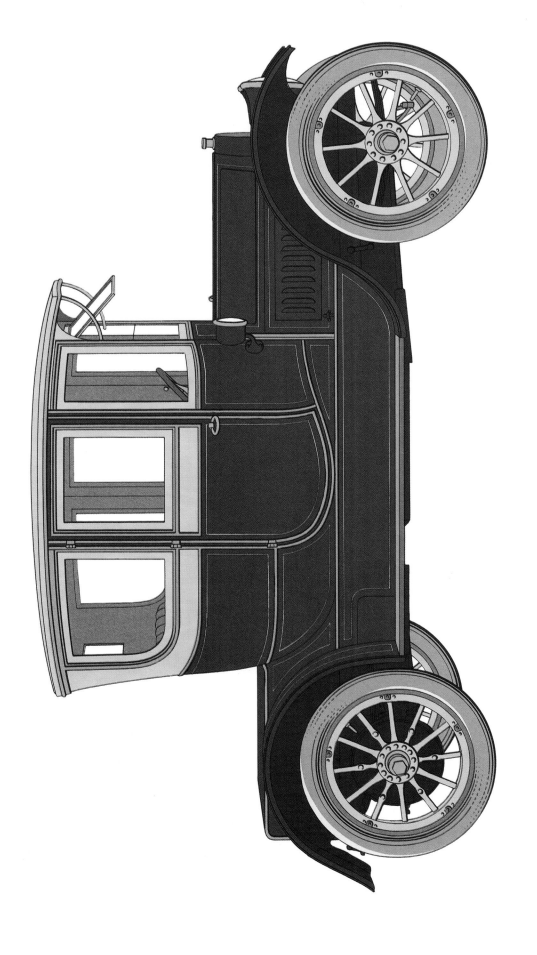

*Cadillac Coupé 1913*

PLATE 91

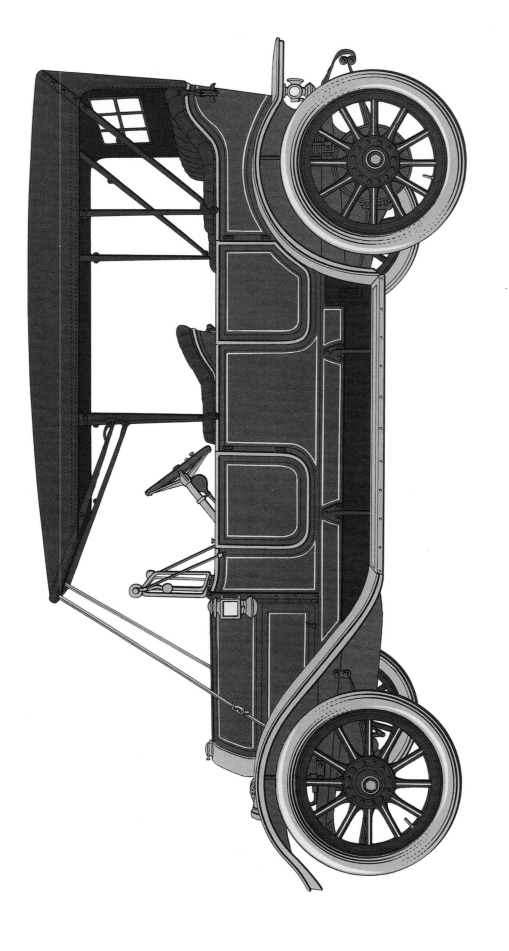

Overland "69" Touring Car   1913

PLATE 92

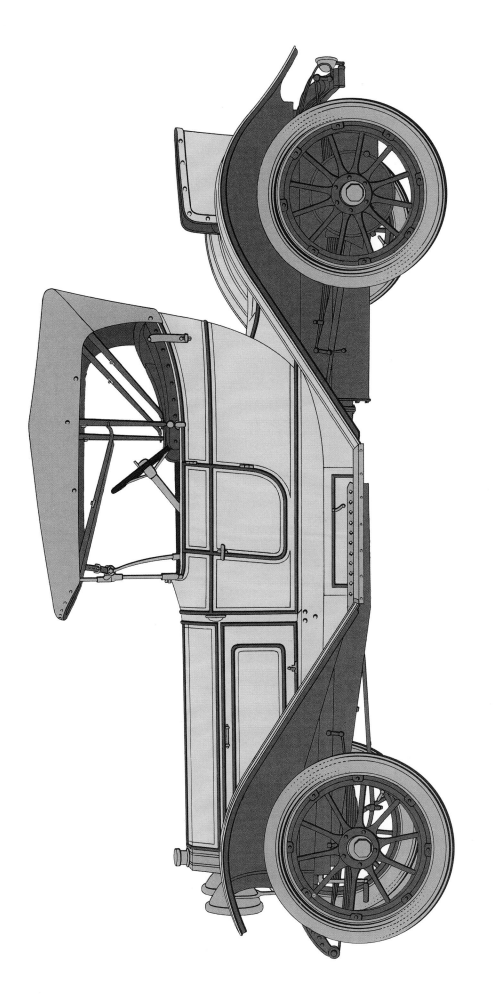

*Peerless Roadster 1913*

PLATE 93

Chevrolet Royal Mail Roadster 1914

PLATE 94

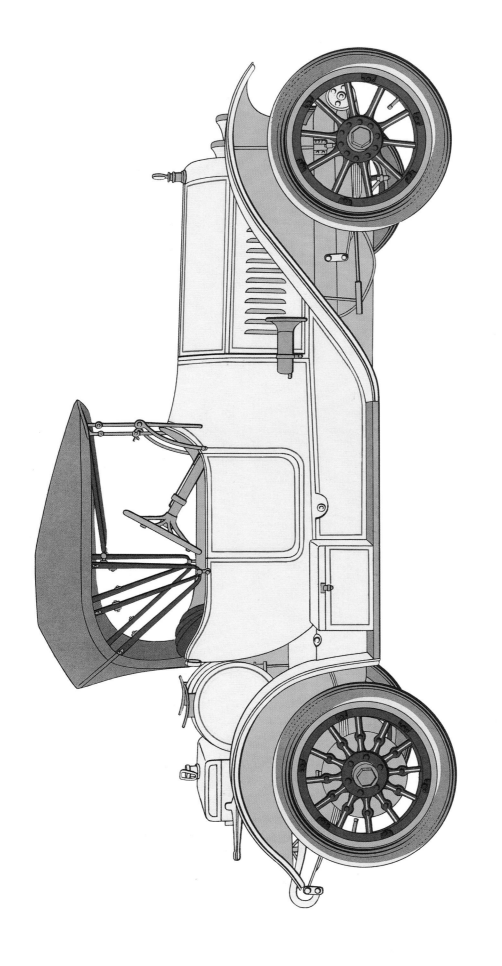

Stutz Bearcat 1914

Plate 95

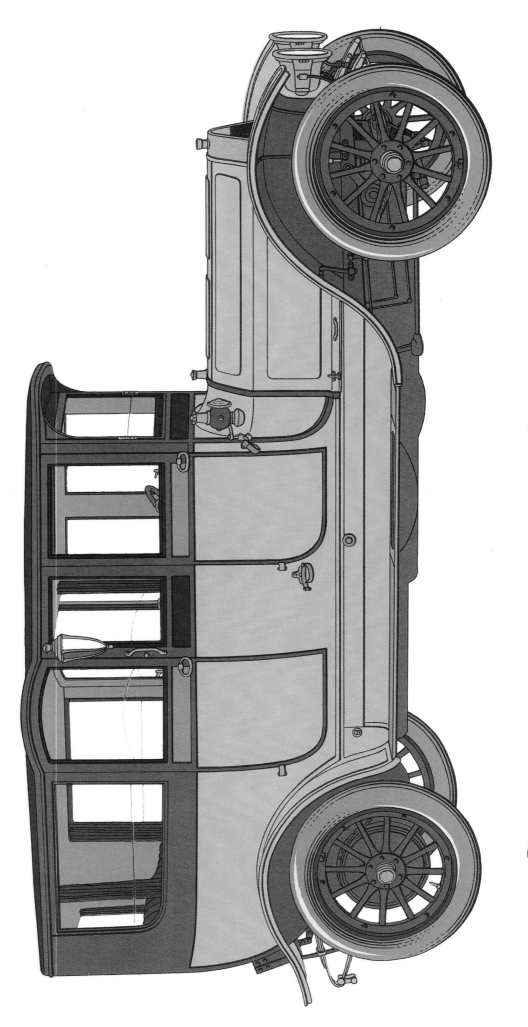

Pierce-Arrow Vestibule Suburban 1914

Plate 96

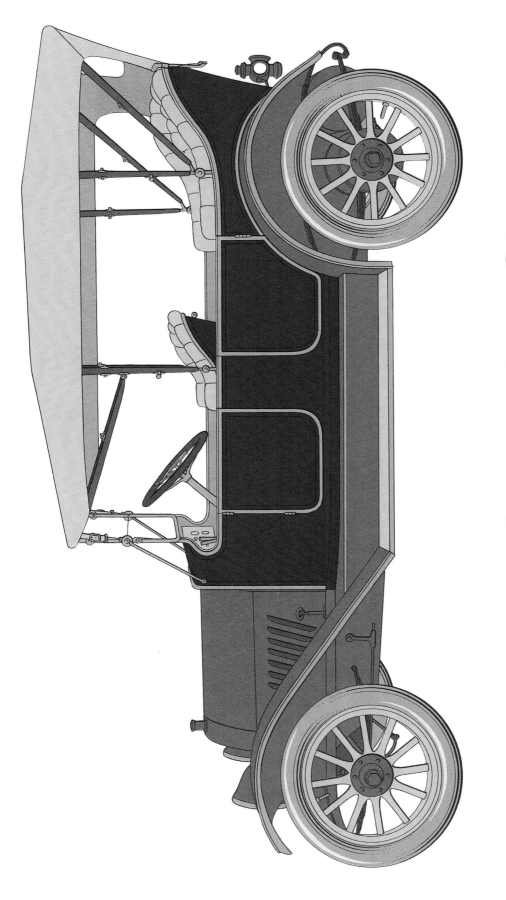

Chevrolet Baby Grand Touring Car   1914

PLATE 97

*Hupmobile "32" Touring Car 1914*

PLATE 98

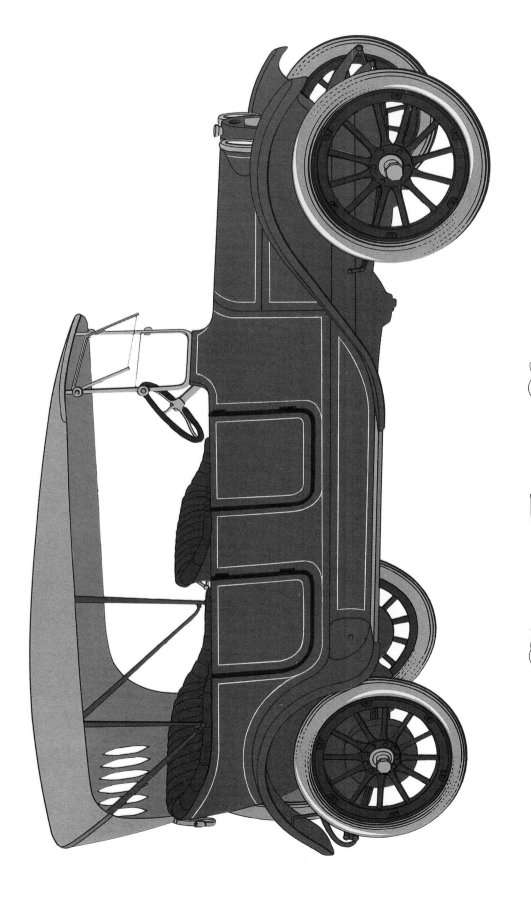

Dodge Touring Car   1914

PLATE 99

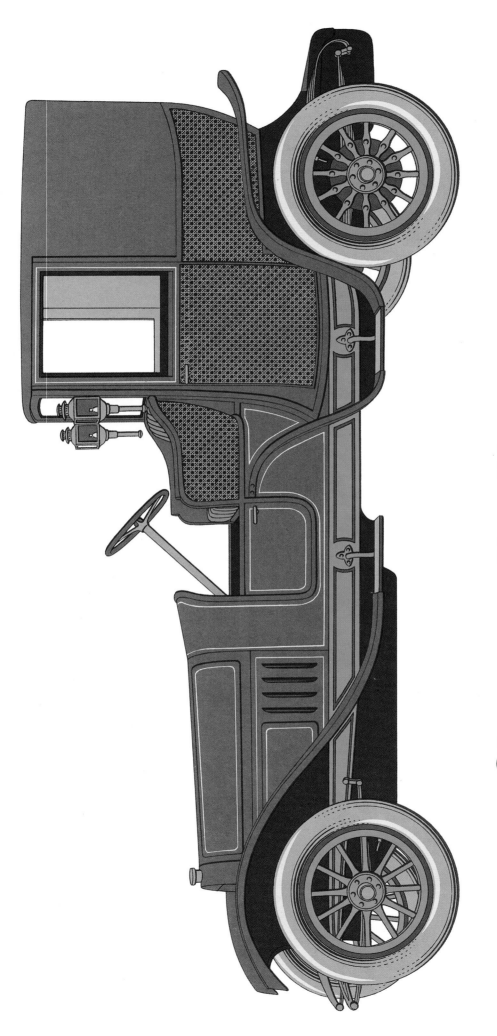

Locomobile Town Coupé   1915

PLATE 100

## PLATE 1: Dudgeon Steam Wagon, 1853

From almost the beginning of recorded history the vision of a vehicle, "self-moved, obedient to the beck of gods" has stirred the imagination of man. These dreams did not become a reality, however, until man learned to harness the power of steam. Richard Dudgeon, of New York, was one of the first Americans to solve the problem. Around 1853 he built the steam wagon shown here. It was virtually a railroad locomotive with unflanged wheels, adapted to road travel. Dudgeon's wagon was reportedly capable of 10 miles per hour on roads of the day and was believed to be fitted with two 3 × 16 inch cylinders. Unfortunately this historic vehicle was destroyed in the Crystal Palace fire and very few technical details are known about it. We can surmise though that a strong fireman and a good stock of coal must have been standard equipment since reliable liquid fuel was still to be developed. Dudgeon maintained that in 1866–67 he built a duplicate of the 1853 steam wagon. This later model is still in existence today and is housed at the Larz Anderson Museum in Brookline, Mass. It has four solid wooden wheels, a steam engine up front and can seat 10 people on the parallel benches running the seven foot length of the boiler.

## PLATE 2: Roper Steam Carriage, 1863

Sylvester H. Roper of Roxbury, Mass. began his experiments as early as 1859. Even though the Civil War was claiming most of America's energy in the middle 1860's, the automobile idea was still kept alive by a few inventors such as Roper. The building of his first steam vehicle is generally credited with being sometime in 1863. It was a conventional four-wheel carriage with room for two passengers and enough coal stored under the seat for a day's use. A 16-inch boiler was placed under the seat with the water tank at the rear. Roper's engine is estimated to have developed around 2 h.p. It was a 2-cylinder affair and had each of its 2 cylinders operating independent of each other through sliding rods to cranks on the inner ends of each side. The need for a differential gear was thereby eliminated. The Roper carriage was exhibited extensively at fairs in the area by a "Professor" W. W. Austin. Handbills publicizing the showings have been preserved and in them can be seen Roper's challenge to match his carriage "against any trotting horse in the world." Many other steam vehicles were built by Roper until his death in 1896—attributed to a heart attack while testing one of his steam bicycles.

## PLATE 3: Carhart Steam Wagon, 1871

With steam, smoke and noise rising from its short smokestack, as well as an occasional blast of fire 10 or 15 feet high, the "Spark" was indeed a terrifying sight. It made its first trip at 10 miles an hour down the hitherto quiet streets of Racine, Wis. early in September, 1871. Dr. W. W. Carhart, its builder, related that it was not long before both the citizens of Racine and the horses were giving him undisputed right of way. A physician and an ordained Methodist minister, Dr. Carhart had conceived the idea for his steam vehicle after building a small steam launch in 1868–1869. It closely resembled some of the early locomotives with its small, upright boiler and two slide-valve engines, all mounted on high, steel-tired buggy wheels four or five feet in diameter. The boiler held about 20 gallons of water and could operate under pressure as high as 200 pounds. Carhart estimated that his 2½ × 3" engines developed around four horsepower. Each drove its wheel independently. Two trains of reducing gears were used to transmit power and the engines were fitted with link motion; this permitted reversing. Shortly after its completion the vehicle, nicknamed "The Spark," was dismantled and used as a power plant for a printing establishment run by the inventor's son.

## PLATE 4: Selden Road Wagon, 1877

The Selden road wagon shown here was, in a way, the cause célèbre of one of the most heated and prolonged patent cases ever aired in an American courtroom. Part of the controversy stemmed from the fact that this vehicle was actually built many years after 1877, though its inventor claimed that the design-concept dated from 1877. George B. Selden was a young patent attorney in Rochester, N.Y. with highly developed mechanical aptitudes. In 1879 he applied for a patent on a self-propelled vehicle; by 1895 such a patent had been granted him. It discloses an automobile with all the basic components of a modern motor car: a body, running and steering gear, clutch, power shaft and liquid fuel tank. The novelty lay in the combination of these units with a 2-cycle, Brayton-type engine using liquid hydrocarbon fuel. In 1903 the holders of the Selden Patent rights sued the Ford Motor Company claiming that Ford was infringing on their patent rights. During the course of the trial this vehicle was built using the specifications delineated in Selden's original patent-application. The vehicle ran briefly. Finally in 1911 the court ruled that Ford was not in violation, that the Selden patent covered only cars powered by 2-cycle engines.

## PLATE 5: Copeland Steam Tricycle, 1886

Early in the 1890's America seemed quite willing to accept the idea of a steam-driven car. Much of the credit for this readiness can be directly attributed to early pioneers such as Lucius D. Copeland whose efforts were publicized through exhibitions and the journals of the day. Copeland, a resident of Phoenix, Arizona, built his first machine around 1884. It was a Star bicycle with a high four or five foot wheel in the rear and a much smaller one in front. A small engine and a vertical boiler at the front supplied about ½ h.p. Two years later his 1886 steam tricycle appeared. This seemed much more practical and better engineered than his first effort. The driver operated the machine from the rear while another passenger sat in front; both were protected from the sun and the rain by a dainty fringed top. The tricycle was powered by a tiny two-cylinder engine. Again, a vertical copper and brass boiler with a safety valve and glass water gauge was used. This time, however, Copeland mounted it in the rear. The entire machine weighed about 185 pounds. Pedals were left on the tricycle so the driver could assist the engine when extra power was needed for climbing hills or making sudden spurts.

## PLATE 6: Morrison-Sturgis Electric, 1890

William Morrison of Des Moines was reputedly a "quiet, mysterious man." He was educated in a Scottish university and by the time he arrived in Iowa he had become a vegetarian, a chemist and a man intensely interested in electricity. The creation of an automobile was of little concern to him in building this vehicle; rather, he wished to prove the worth of his storage batteries. In the summer of 1890 Morrison began installing batteries in a surrey-type, high-wheel carriage. It was a stock model with fringed canopy top and three rows of cushioned seats able to accommodate 12 passengers. A set of eight batteries was placed under each seat. The power was applied through a modified Siemens armature geared direct to the right rear wheel. Around 2½ h.p., sufficient to drive the carriage 6 to 7 mph, could be developed. The vehicle ran on the streets of Des Moines in September 1890 and in 1891 was given to the American Battery Company of Chicago for demonstration purposes. Harold Sturgis, secretary of the Chicago concern, showed the carriage extensively and it became the most widely known self-propelled vehicle in America. In 1895 Sturgis installed a different motor in Morrison's electric and entered it in the Times-Herald race.

## PLATE 7: Nadig Road Wagon, 1891

With the wane of the 19th century, the motor age in America began slowly to dawn. Now the machines of a handful of inventors scattered throughout the Midwest and East began taking to the roads. These first efforts were crude and unreliable at best. However, they ran and more important, they were gasoline-driven! One such pioneer builder was Henry Nadig, of Allentown, Pa., an immigrant German machinist. Nadig testified in 1905 at the Selden Patent Trial that he had never seen nor heard of a gasoline-powered carriage before building his own. He began with a single-cylinder 4½ × 6″ engine that was water-jacketed for cooling. The four-cycle engine and its double flywheel weighed around 300 pounds and was strapped to two hickory beams at the rear of the carriage. Nadig placed a gasoline tank near the dash. Felt and wire gauze acted as vaporizing agents with the gas being drawn to the engine through a ¼-inch suction pipe. There it was ignited by a tube kept hot with the flame from a Bunsen burner. Though the engine was rated at only around 8 h.p., speeds of up to 15 mph were attained. The Nadig car was frequently seen in 1891 on runs around Allentown and on the Coopertown Pike.

## PLATE 8: Lambert Gasoline Buggy, 1891

In the light of present-day evidence many automotive historians are now inclined to credit John W. Lambert with the development of America's first gasoline automobile. Lambert's historic car is believed to have been road tested in Ohio City, Ohio in January or February 1891. While the vehicle has long since disappeared, there are sworn statements and a photograph in the Smithsonian Institution indicating that the car was ridden in and photographed in 1891. Lightness seemed to be Lambert's aim in designing his little three-wheeler. The fringed-top carriage was specially constructed in Cleveland with a two-passenger, spindle-seated body. Lambert used a single-cylinder (3½ × 4″), four-cycle engine that was water-cooled by a three-gallon tank. A single vaporizer drew air past the gasoline and produced the right mixture for firing by the make and break ignition. Power was transmitted by chain to a rear axle equipped with a bevel gear type differential. While forward speeds up to 15 miles per hour were claimed for the car, no provisions were made for reversing. Lambert's steering arrangement was particularly novel with the driver having both a foot lever and hand lever at his disposal. Either one could be used to guide the machine.

## PLATE 9: Schloemer-Toepfer Carriage, 1892

The first recorded race in the U.S. between self-propelled vehicles occurred in Wisconsin in 1878. In that year two steam machines left Green Bay in quest of a $10,000 prize offered by the Wisconsin state legislature. It is quite possible that Gottfried Schloemer's interest in the horseless carriage was spurred on by the publicity given this 200-mile race. Schloemer's cooperage shop in Milwaukee was the scene of many spirited discussions between him and his friend, Frank Toepfer, a locksmith. According to a former employee of Toepfer, the two men "would discuss the auto for hours—they would get a bucket of beer and talk and sketch." Their historic vehicle finally took to the streets in 1892. Its maiden journey up West Water Street left dozens of frightened horses and curious onlookers in its wake. Schloemer and Toepfer used an ordinary top buggy with special wooden wheels covered with hard rubber for their chassis. The motive power came from a 1-cylinder, 2-cycle gasoline engine of 3½-inch bore and stroke. Two points of steel striking together ignited the gas while current was supplied from wet batteries. Two men usually rode in the car, one to push if necessary. The car is now in the Milwaukee Public Museum.

## PLATE 10: Duryea Gasoline Buggy, 1893

J. Frank Duryea died in 1967; until then he had been one of the few living pioneers whose experiences went back to the very beginning of the horseless carriage era in America. He and his brother, Charles E., 1861-1938, share the honor of building this vehicle, one of the earliest forerunners of today's modern motor car. It was constructed in Russell's Machine Shop in Springfield, Mass. and in September of 1893 was driven on the streets of that city. A phaeton buggy comprised the body and chassis and a sailboat type tiller was utilized for steering. The two-passenger carriage was driven by a four-horsepower, one-cylinder, water-cooled engine. With two forward gears and one reverse—shifted by moving the tiller up and down—the vehicle could go almost 15 miles per hour on its iron-strapped wheels. One of the Duryea's more advanced

features was a spray carburetor, an essential in all modern-day cars. Charles stated that he was inspired to invent it by his wife's perfume atomizer. A heated controversy raged for decades over which of the Duryea brothers should be credited with developing the car. After many years of careful research the Automobile Old Timers Association ruled that both brothers deserve equal credit. In 1921 the Duryea was placed in the Smithsonian where it may be seen today.

## PLATE 11: Black Gasoline Carriage, 1893

The long roll call of Hoosier-made automobiles begins with this primitive, 1893 gasoline buggy built by Charles H. Black. Black operated a wagon works and smithy in Indianapolis and was well known as a carriage-maker. His long-standing interest in self-propelled vehicles had been particularly stirred by an 1891 Benz a friend of his had imported from Germany and allowed Black to drive. In 1892 he began construction of his own machine. It was completed the following year and there is little doubt that many features of the Black car were inspired by the Benz. Black used an ordinary buggy for the body, wood carriage wheels and solid rubber tires. The engine was a one-cylinder, four-cycle type with an automatic inlet valve, open crankcase and exposed crankshaft. It was started by pushing the machine or by turning the flywheel by hand. Ignition was by kerosene torch and two belts led from the engine to a jackshaft. They were driven by two different-sized pulleys on the crankshaft, providing a high and a low speed. Black's car was frequently seen in the 1890's on the streets of Indianapolis. Today it fittingly rests in a place of honor in the Children's Museum of that city.

## PLATE 12: Haynes Gasoline Carriage, 1894

On a bright 4th of July afternoon in 1894, Elwood Haynes had this strange-looking buggy without tongue or shafts towed out from the city to a country road. Then to the amazement of onlookers he drove it back triumphantly into Kokomo, Ind. at the remarkable speed of seven miles an hour under power generated by a gasoline engine. It was the result of two years' experimentation by Haynes and was partly inspired by a desire to find a more rapid way of making his rounds over the large territory he covered as a superintendent. He had purchased a one-horsepower Sintz upright marine engine and had brought this and his plans to Apperson Brothers' shop in the winter of 1893-94. The engine was mounted vertically in a chassis made of a double hollow square of steel tubing. Sprocket wheels to transmit the engine power to the rear wheels by means of ordinary bicycle chains did not exist at the time and were specially designed. Being without a starting mechanism, the car had to be pushed before the engine would catch. In 1922 a memorial tablet was erected on the Pumpkinvine Pike three miles southeast of Kokomo. It designates the exact spot where Haynes first set the car in motion under its own power.

## PLATE 13: Morris & Salom Electrobat, 1895

The electric carriage which Pedro Salom and Henry Morris entered in the Chicago Times-Herald Race of 1895 was their second vehicle. (An earlier one had appeared on the streets of Philadelphia in August, 1894.) Caffery of Camden, N.J. had built the body for this model. It was a two-seated affair with spindled sides, tufted leather upholstery and an abbreviated buckboard. Each drive wheel carried a 1½ h.p. Lundell 80-volt motor. Though the body weighed slightly less than 1000 pounds, another 669 pounds were added when batteries were installed. The makers claimed a maximum speed of 20 mph and maintained that a range of 25 miles could be expected on a single charge. Because of the heavy snow on the day of the race the Electrobat could not finish; still the judges awarded it a gold medal because it was "clean, easy to drive and there were neither noise, smell, heat nor vibration." Two very unusual features should be noted: with its motors attached to the front wheels, it was one of our earliest front wheel drive cars; it also had the added fascination of rear wheel steering.

## PLATE 14: Holtzer-Cabot Electric, 1895

From the time of its first inception, the electric car never departed very far from its coach-building tradition. The Holtzer-Cabot is a prime example, a vehicle whose principal accents were comfort, smoothness of operation and simplicity of control. This wagon, built on commission from a wealthy resident of Boston, clearly follows the design of the English break coach. It weighed 5100 pounds and was powered by 44 chloride cell batteries capable of producing speeds of five, eight and fifteen miles per hour. These were operated by the lever shown alongside the steering shaft. A notched arc and spring latch locked the mechanism in the various speed positions. The makers built the carriage as water-tight as possible and covered it with liberal amounts of acid-proof paint; if a cell were to break and spill acid no damage would result to the motor or its connections directly underneath the batteries. Shiny cut-glass lamps of 10 candlepower each, distinctively elegant step plates and leather upholstery tooled by experienced craftsmen, gave the Holtzer-Cabot as smart an appearance as any horse-drawn "turn-out" of the 1890's.

## PLATE 15: Duryea Motor Wagon, 1895

America's first publicized road race was run over the snow-covered streets of Chicago on Thanksgiving day in 1895. This car, driven by J. Frank Duryea, won the 54-mile race with an average speed of 7½ miles per hour. Six cars faced the starting gun with the Duryea entry being the overwhelming favorite. It was lighter and less cumbersome than any of the others, weighing only 750 pounds when fully gassed. From the time of its competition it had travelled hundreds of miles in demonstrations in and around Springfield, Mass. The Duryea brothers had built an earlier vehicle but this was a new design throughout. Instead of combining a ready-built carriage body with an engine, they had started from scratch and fashioned a special body, 33 inches wide and 18 inches deep at the rear. Under the flooring a water tank was placed. Water was circulated from the tank through the engine jackets by a pump operated by an eccentric on the engine shaft. Particular care had been taken to conceal the engine within the body and the trim effect of the finished car was a startling contrast with their earlier effort. Its two-cycle engine was rated at only four horsepower at 500 rpm's; yet its capacity was much greater at 700 rpm's, a speed it easily reached.

## PLATE 16: Ford Quadricycle, 1896

Though steam had really been Henry Ford's first love, he soon decided that the future lay with gasoline engines. The Quadricycle was his first car and in it can be seen one striking quality which anticipated later Ford practice—it weighed only 500 pounds and was the lightest vehicle of its type yet produced. Also apparent is the strong influence of the bicycle. Bicycle wheels and steel-tube chassis were used and even a bicycle saddle was fitted on top of the three-gallon fuel tank. (The two-passenger buggy seat came later when more funds were available.) Three years of experimentation preceded the car and it was not until June of 1896 that it was trundled out of its shop at 58 Bagley Avenue for a trial spin. A four-cycle, two-cylinder engine put together from discarded scrap-metal bits and a plumber's pipe, generated about three to four horsepower. Two belts were arranged to transmit the engine's power to the drive wheels. A clutch lever tightened or loosened the belts and gave the driver the choice of 10 or 20 mph speeds. The car was a crude machine by modern standards—yet it ran, and it was soon to be joined by millions of its descendants.

## PLATE 17: King Horseless Carriage, 1896

Detroit's first glimpse of the horseless carriage occurred on the night of March 6, 1896 when Charles B. King rolled his handmade automobile out of a machine shop on St. Antoine St. and drove it to Cadillac Square. The wagon had been loaned to King by a Cincinnati firm interested in the future of self-propelled vehicles. In the chassis he installed his own four-cycle, four-cylinder motor, a type which would become standard on later cars. It had a 2¾ × 5¾ inch bore and stroke and was completely open—both the crankshaft and bottoms of the pistons were exposed. Since there was no crankcase, there was no oiling system and each bearing had to be oiled by hand from an oil can. A foot-operated accelerator, a muffler and gasoline and water tanks were added. King had already worked out designs for steering wheels but when the Cincinnati wagon came equipped with a tiller, he merely rebuilt and improved it. In 1956 a replica of the King car was constructed from original blueprints and presented to the Detroit Historical Museum. After the historic run King remained active in automotive circles, later designing and manufacturing the once-famous Northern and King cars.

## PLATE 18: Mueller Motor Carriage, 1897

Hieronymus Mueller was an early automotive pioneer of Decatur, Ill. who literally gave his life to his interest. In 1895 he had entered a modified Benz wagon in the epochal Thanksgiving Day Race in Chicago and finished second. This, his third car, was completed in 1897; three years later Mueller was killed in a gasoline explosion while developing yet another automobile. For the body of his 1897 machine he selected a handsome carriage in the style of a trap. Its dos-à-dos seating, wood-spoked wheels and high flaring mudguards were left unchanged. However, a four-cycle, two-cylinder engine of 4 h.p. was installed and a condenser for cooling water placed on the front of the leather dash. With these improvements, and a combination of gears and chains, the jaunty little rig could now develop speeds from 3 to 20 miles per hour "on ordinary roads." Pneumatic tires, Hyatt roller bearings, brass oil lamps and a strident bulb horn were early-day concessions to the comfort as well as the safety of passengers. A few years later Mueller's son recalled a trip he and his father had taken from Decatur to Indianapolis in 1895 in the Mueller car. "Bicyclists, farmers, barefooted boys pursued the machine, scarcely able to realize that it could move under its own power."

## PLATE 19: Olds Motor Carriage, 1897

Ransom Eli Olds was a pioneer within a select group of inventive geniuses whose mechanical skill, resourcefulness and promotional daring helped usher in the motor age. The Olds Motor Vehicle Company signed papers of incorporation at Lansing on August 21, 1897 and Olds was immediately directed to build "one carriage in as nearly perfect a manner as possible." This motor vehicle and three others like it were completed in that year. It was a typical chain-driven machine and carried four passengers on its hard rubber tires. The dash was angular, clearly of buggy origin. Though the body had come from a Lansing carriage factory, Olds and his co-worker, Frank Clark, labored many hours to adapt it for self-propelled travel. A special front axle was devised to facilitate steering; changes were necessary in the spring suspension and drive, and an extra seat was added. It was driven by a six-horsepower, single-cylinder, water-cooled engine capable of producing a 10 mph speed. A small device, consisting of a battery coil and a primitive spark plug made from a water glass, produced the necessary spark for combustion of the gas. One sole survivor of the four 1897 Oldsmobiles remains; it is now in the Smithsonian Institution.

## PLATE 20: Autocar Phaeton, 1898

This phaeton carriage was the second car made by Louis S. Clarke, founder of the Autocar Company and one of the early auto industry's most brilliant engineers. For many years it slowly gathered dust in an out-of-the-way loft, neglected and almost forgotten. Then one day it was unearthed and with loving care, restored to mint condition by the man who had originally built it, Mr. Clarke. In 1954 it was presented to the Henry Ford Museum in Dearborn, Mich. Autocar No. 2 is a trim little rig, lighted by oil lamps and mounted on sulky wheels. Clarke was an early advocate of the left-hand drive and placed his tiller steering device in a position where the drive would be on the side nearest to approaching vehicles. A foot-operated bell to signal traffic was added. Two horizontal cylinders of 3¾-inch bore and 4-inch stroke are located under the seat and can drive the carriage at top speeds of 15 mph. The lever on the left provides two forward speeds; there is no reverse. It is difficult to realize that this dainty, 900-pound phaeton, with its 55-inch wheelbase, is the forerunner of the huge trucks which now bear the Autocar nameplate.

## PLATE 21: Woods Electric Hansom, 1898

Long before Woods' electric cabs appeared in Chicago, horse-drawn hansoms of almost identical appearance had been carrying passengers through the streets of the larger cities of the world. Woods' electric retained the classic perch set high in the rear. From this vantage point the driver had an excellent view of traffic and could readily spot prospective fares. A tiller steering arrangement, with switches on the pillar allowing speeds of either 3, 6 or 12 mph, made the 2600-pound cab easy to operate. Two forward-swinging doors opened to allow passenger entry into the richly upholstered interior equipped with electric foot warmers; electricity also lighted the side lanterns. Though passengers did not travel at great speeds, their ride was noiseless. This was one of the advantages electric car advocates liked to point out at the turn of the century. They also emphasized the electric's lack of odor—a common complaint against gasoline engines with their imperfect combustion. On the other hand, a vehicle of the Woods type could run only 30 miles on one charge. It took at least three hours to recharge the batteries and recharging stations were found only in the bigger cities. Woods' hansom was powered by two 3½ h.p. engines and cost $3050.

## PLATE 22: Ford Gasoline Carriage, 1898

Late in 1896, Henry Ford began work on a second car. He envisioned a machine with a sturdier chassis, more passenger room and stronger wheels, and one in which most of the machinery could be enclosed. Improvements should be made in the motor and a better transmission system was a must. The 1898 result represented a major advance toward these goals. It was a typical auto buggy, outfitted with patent-leather fenders, brass kerosene lamps and special reinforced bicycle wheels—trim and finished looking. It was seven feet long, weighed 875 pounds and, unlike its predecessor, had a reverse and a neutral gear. A gear type arrangement for the transmission of power had replaced the conventional chain and sprocket type, thus allowing the engine's power to be transmitted directly to the rear axle. By means of a newly perfected carburetor, the flow of gasoline was regulated so that only the exact amount necessary entered the motor. There it was ignited by an electric spark. This feature would practically eliminate bad odors caused by uncombusted gasoline, Ford claimed. Though this car is but one link in a long chain of experimental models, it is historically significant; in it can be seen the faint beginning of Ford's dream of a superior, practical, low-cost car for America.

## PLATE 23: Winton Motor Carriage, 1898

On the strength of the performance shown in a spectacular 800-mile trip from Cleveland to New York, in 1897, The Winton Motor Carriage Company was established. The sale of a Winton in early 1898 is believed to represent the first instance of a bona-fide sale of an American-built gasoline automobile manufactured on a regular production basis. By the end of the year, Alexander Winton had delivered 22 machines in all, priced at $1000 each. Their 1898 models were handsome little carriages. By housing the motor and most of the machinery inside the body, an exceptionally clean look had been achieved. The company claimed that its single-cylinder engine, horizontally placed, would take the machine "anywhere a horse and trap can be negotiated." The engine's most distinctive feature was its quality of speed variation; this enabled it to run from 200 to 1000 rpm's with any range between attainable in a few seconds. Gear changing was necessary only on steep hills or for reversing. The speed of the engine was controlled by a spring button located on the floor board. With chain drive, ball bearings on all axles and tires advertised as "practically puncture proof," the car was well worth the money and only a small portion of the orders received could be filled.

## PLATE 24: Riker Electric Tricycle, 1898

It is interesting to note that Riker's 1898 vehicle incorporated not one but two features which fell into disfavor at an early date but are again being seriously considered by modern-day car designers—a three-wheel chassis and electrical power. Andrew L. Riker had constructed an electric tricycle in the 1880's. However, it was not until 1898 that this model, produced in Brooklyn, N.Y., was placed on the market. Riker employed a triangular, tubular steel frame that was the essence of simplicity. It offered many advantages, the primary ones being weight reduction, ease of handling and low manufacturing costs. The two-passenger tricycle had a black wooden body, black leather fenders and 28-inch bicycle tires fitted with 2½" pneumatic tires. It weighed 800 pounds and had a four-foot tread and four-foot wheelbase. A small ¾ k.w., 40-volt motor weighing 60 pounds was attached to the rear wheel. By pushing the controller lever ahead three forward speeds (3, 6 and 11 mph) could be attained. A foot-operated electric bell was provided, and to thwart would-be thieves, the batteries could be disconnected by means of a lock switch under the seat. An 1898 Riker tricycle is now on display at the Henry Ford Museum.

## PLATE 25: Packard Model "A", 1899

The first Packard was built by a young arc-light magnate of Warren, Ohio largely as an expression of his dissatisfaction with a Winton he had recently purchased. James Ward Packard christened his machine the Model "A," as if

sensing that it was only the first of a long, long line. Its buggy ancestry was plainly evident in the leather fenders and dash, buttoned-leather upholstery and even a whip-socket. However, the first trial run proved the car to be both tough and versatile with plenty of ground clearance to take it over the deeply rutted roads of the day. The shovel-handled tiller guided the machine as it whizzed along at speeds up to 30 miles an hour. Its engine, a single-cylinder, 12-horsepower type, was placed horizontally under the seat. An opening on the right-hand side of the body allowed access to the engine and served as a place to insert the crank. One of the more advanced features of the engine was an automatic spark control. This eliminated the need of the driver having to hurry around and personally retard the spark after cranking. In 1927 Packard presented the Model "A" to his alma mater, Lehigh University, where it is now preserved.

## PLATE 26: Columbia Daumon Victoria, 1899

Between 1895 and 1900 a number of makers produced electric cars on a commercial basis; one of the most successful was the Columbia Electric. Preliminary design sketches of the Daumon Victoria had been prepared as early as 1897 but it was not until 1899 that one designed by William Hooker Atwood was produced by the Columbia and Electric Vehicle Company at its Hartford, Conn. plant. Atwood's design conformed very closely to the conventional Victoria carriage type but was unique in the addition of Daumon boxes to carry the batteries; half were located over the front axle, the others over the rear axle. The Mark V Victoria is sometimes regarded as the most elegant equipage ever produced. When President Roosevelt visited Hartford a carriage of this type was used to convey him on his tour of the city. The vehicle was operated from the driver's seat at the rear overlooking the passenger compartment. Along with the controls the rear seat could also accommodate a footman. Columbia's Mark V attained a speed of approximately 12 miles per hour and on a level terrain about 30 miles. Two motors geared to the rear axle powered this 3250-pound carriage. It had 3" pneumatic tires, front wheels of 32" and rear wheels of 36".

## PLATE 27: Locomobile Steamer, 1899

In 1897 the twin brothers Francis E. and Freelan O. Stanley put a steam engine in a car and created a legend. They sold their business in 1899 to a New England firm which manufactured and marketed the Stanley-developed machine under the name of Locomobile. The 1899 stanhope model weighed 800 pounds and sold for $750. It was well engineered, amazingly efficient and relatively simple in its mechanical conception. Essential components were few: a three-gallon gasoline tank under the floor boards; a 16-gage seamless copper boiler, 14 inches in diameter and 14 inches deep, directly under the driver's seat; under the boiler, a sheet-metal burner with 114 short vertical tubes which acted as Bunsen burners; and finally, the means of conveying the power of the steam to the rear wheels, a 2-cylinder locomotive type engine placed slightly to the front of the boiler. The car accelerated rapidly once set in motion by a lever to the driver's right. A foot pedal operated the brake and if a speedier stop were desired, the engine could be reversed. Though Locomobile abandoned steam cars in 1901, the Star.ley brothers continued stubbornly yet brilliantly to build steam-driven vehicles with complete disregard for the growing competition of the gasoline engine.

## PLATE 28: Knox Three-Wheeler, 1899

The 1899 car designed by Harry A. Knox of Springfield, Mass. boasted several noteworthy features. It had a wishbone-shaped, angle-iron frame that was one of the sturdiest of its day. It also had the distinction of being one of the first cars to use an air-cooled engine. Large numbers of threaded rods, ⅛ inch in diameter, were screwed into the cylinder walls, tremendously increasing the amount of cooling surface. Knox's "porcupine" engine was a one-cylinder type with bore and stroke of 4½ × 6 inches. Two speeds were provided but no reverse, since the vehicle could turn in a nine-foot circle. As the driver sat in the stanhope style body the steering wheel faced him and two levers were on his left. One of the levers controlled the engine clutch and the speed gear; the other regulated the speed of the engine. The Knox was capable of 25 mph with the gear ordinarily furnished; a special racing gear to increase this speed was offered. Before its demise in 1913–1914, the Knox Company became one of America's largest manufacturers of commercial vehicles. It supplied customers with delivery vans, drays, police patrols, fire wagons, hotel and passenger buses and many other vehicles.

## PLATE 29: Riker Electric Brougham, 1900

A. L. Riker was one of the earliest builders of electric racing cars. On April 14, 1900 a Riker machine defeated 9 other vehicles in the Merrick road race on Long Island with an average speed of about 25 miles per hour. His firm, the Riker Motor Company of Elizabethville, N.J., produced a great variety of vehicles both for passenger transportation and the delivery of goods. The broughams were the most luxurious of their entire line and were made on special order for customers in London, Paris and the U.S. With the interior richly upholstered, carpeted and boasting an electric reading lamp, a speaking tube for communication with the chauffeur, a coach clock and a receiving rack to hold miscellaneous personal items, the brougham's appointments were indeed sumptuous. Four passengers, two facing forward and two to the rear, could be seated in the wooden body. Its frame was depressed so as to permit a low floor and, according to the company's advertisement, an efficient suspension system assured a ride that was without vibration. With two Electric Vehicle Company motors geared to the rear axle, the Riker was capable of a speed of about 12 miles per hour. It weighed around 4000 pounds and had an 89″ wheelbase and a 56″ tread.

## PLATE 30: Woods Station Wagon, 1900

By 1900 almost every form of horse-drawn pleasure carriage had been duplicated in the electric car. C. E. Woods of Chicago alone produced over 30 different body types in that year. His advertising emphasized the desirability of choosing the correct style of livery for the purpose intended. The station wagon shown here was a conveyance proper families would be proud to own for theatre use. Its clean silent elegance would also make it suitable for a quiet spin up fashionable Lake Shore Drive, or through Chicago's parks and boulevards. It weighed 2600 pounds and was fitted with two-inch hard rubber tires and painted wooden wheels measuring 36 inches in front and 42 in the rear. Woods used a 3½-horsepower motor at each rear wheel. These were built with ironclad armatures and special coil windings that were wound before being placed on the armature. The single lever to the left of the driver served a dual purpose. It controlled the speed of the vehicle, up to 12 miles per hour, and applied the brakes. Electric lights were standard equipment and like most electric cars, it had an electric bell to warn traffic. (Raucous horns were left to the gasoline machines.) Price, $2350 not including crating and cartage.

## PLATE 31: Columbia Electric Phaeton, 1900

This stylish and attractive Columbia Electric phaeton was in every sense a "gentleman's carriage" as its designer, William Atwood, intended it to be. It was made in Hartford, Conn.; in time it came to be generally recognized as almost a standard type of American electric vehicle. Most of its lines were sharp and straight. Atwood dismissed rounded edges as trademarks of the vulgar "Western buggy school of architecture." A neat detachable rumble seat at the rear and a large hooded top were standard equipment along with durable wulfing cloth upholstery. The carriage was driven by a rear-mounted single 25-ampere motor connected with two driving shafts. With a total weight of 2650 pounds, this phaeton was surprisingly light when it is realized that over 1100 pounds of this was accounted for by its 44-cell chloride battery. The phaeton's wheelbase measured 65 inches, tread 54 inches. Three forward speeds of 3, 6 and 12 mph and two reverse speeds were possible. Shiny patent leather fenders, step plates on either side and trim wire suspension wheels (36″ rear, 32″ front) added to the Columbia's smart appearance.

## PLATE 32: Haynes-Apperson Surrey, 1901

This illustration of the 1901 Haynes-Apperson surrey captures the horseless carriage at one of the most charming moments in its development. It was still a well-made, handsome carriage with no outward pretenses of aspiring to anything else. Soon its straight backboard was to be replaced by a sloping radiator; its spindled seats would give way to solid metal sides; a steering wheel, running boards, tonneaus and a dozen other features would be added as it evolved into modernity. The 1901 Haynes-Apperson's performance, however, belied its carriage appearance. It was powered by an eight-horsepower, two-cylinder engine and the company could point to numerous reliability and endurance contest wins by their 1901 surrey model. The car's engine sat on a steel tubing frame under the seat and was fed a gasoline and air mixture through vaporizers. This mixture was controlled by a foot lever. The Haynes-Apperson Company advised purchasers that their car would go 30 mph and carried enough fuel and water for 150 miles. Other specifications: Three speeds forward, one reverse; muffled exhaust; rawhide gears; oil headlight; 36-inch wooden wheels; pneumatic tires; price, f.o.b. Kokomo, Ind., $1500 with extension top.

## PLATE 33: Riker Theater Bus, 1901

The Theater Bus, as manufactured by the Riker company, was ideally adapted to carrying passengers in all sorts of weather. Because of its large glass windows it rapidly gained popularity as an excursion vehicle. Thirteen passengers could be seated inside and there was room on the roof for several additional people. It was a substantial vehicle with a weight of 5500 pounds, 2¼″ solid rubber tires, 58″ tread in front, 68″ in the rear. Two 2-k.w. motors were geared direct to large spur gears on the wheel hubs to provide a maximum speed of 10 miles per hour and a range of 25 miles before recharging. In addition to the steering tiller all Riker electrics were equipped with a lever which controlled the speed. Various speeds were obtained by dividing the batteries into groups and connecting these groups and the two motors in multiple series. By pushing the lever forward one notch a speed of 2 to 3 miles per hour was attained; to the second notch, 6 to 7 miles an hour; to the third notch, 10 miles an hour. By pressing downward on a latch rod located on the same lever, two reverse speeds could be obtained.

## PLATE 34: White Steamer, 1901

The steam era was reaching its zenith in 1901 when the White Sewing Machine Company introduced this light stanhope model priced at $1000. Development of a superior flash boiler had precipitated the Cleveland firm's entry into the automotive field. White's boiler consisted of horizontal tubes into which water was pumped constantly, flashing into steam as driving conditions required. Its principal advantage lay in an ability to get up steam very rapidly; it was cheap to build and little, if any, scale collected on it. Gasoline provided fuel for the boiler, being forced on its way by air pressure developed by a hand pump just to the right of the driver. Also on his right was a throttle lever which controlled the speed of the two-cylinder engine. When the carriage was unoccupied the handle of the throttle could be removed, thus preventing the carriage from being started through carelessness or mischief. A buggy type top, two kerosene head lamps and a tail lamp completed the car's equipment. When storing the car in zero weather, the manufacturers recommended that a covering extending to the axles on all sides be placed over it and the pilot light kept burning.

## PLATE 35: Duryea Phaeton, 1902

Not long after developing their historic 1893 car in Springfield, Mass., the Duryea brothers went their separate ways. By 1902 J. Frank was producing the Stevens-Duryea in Chicopee Falls, Mass. while Charles, in Reading, Pa., was turning out a line of three-cylinder tonneaus, surreys and phaetons of the type shown here. Duryea placed the three, 4½ × 4½″ cylinders under the seat and fed them gasoline through a small float feed carburetor which weighed only a pound. With a rating of 10 h.p., the engine could produce speeds up to 25 mph. Its power was transmitted directly to the live rear axle by chain drive, and an efficient, 14-inch, expanding type brake was fitted on the sprocket on the differential gear to insure safe stopping. The lever in the middle of the front seat not only steered the car but also served as a throttling device and gear change lever. Charles Duryea offered his graceful phaeton body on either a three- or a four-wheel chassis. He candidly admitted in his advertising that he believed the three-wheeler to be superior to the four. With either chassis the phaeton's price was $1250. It weighed about 800 pounds and measured 66 inches at the wheelbase.

## PLATE 36: Packard "F" Tonneau, 1902

The Model F marked the emergence of the Packard from the buggy to the automobile type. It was larger than any of its predecessors and was the first to have wooden wheels, an exposed front radiator, brakes at the rear wheel hub and separate front seats. Its rear-entrance tonneau, a feature imported from France and ideally suited to short-wheelbase bodies, could be removed and the car became a runabout. In their 1902 catalog the company frankly acknowledged the "popular clamor for multiple cylinder engines placed upright in front." However, they defended their single-cylinder, 12-h.p. engine, hung under the driver's seat, on the grounds that it was easy to get at, provided sufficient power and superior handling because of better weight distribution. This was also the first Packard to have three speeds forward—10, 20 and 30 mph—and one reverse. Ignition was by jump spark and timing was automatically controlled. In addition to a steering column, hinged to swing forward and provide easy access, the F was equipped with a set of tools, a pump, extra oil tanks, four-inch herringbone-tread single tires and a pair of kerosene headlamps. Soon after the introduction of this model the company was reorganized and moved from Warren, Ohio to Detroit.

## PLATE 37: Franklin Runabout, 1902

The 1902 Franklin on exhibit in the Smithsonian Institution is one of the earliest air-cooled cars in existence. Two earlier models had been built for the H. H. Franklin Company of Syracuse, N.Y. under the direction of John Wilkinson. However, it was not until the production of this third machine that Wilkinson felt the company had a car which was reliable and would run satisfactorily. The four-cylinder 3½ × 3½ engine, mounted transversely under a hood in the front, was a radical engineering feat in itself. It appeared at a time when most manufacturers were placing their single-cylinder engines in the rear or under the driver's seat. The car had a chassis of wood reinforced by angle iron on the rails. Full elliptic springs, unorthodox but efficient, were used on all four wheels. In one of the first instances of the use of this kind of equipment, an Apple generator supplied the electric current. Throttle and spark control levers were within easy reach on the steering column just below the wheel. A long narrow gas tank ran beneath the right floor boards to the rear of the car and was filled through a hole cut in the floorboards.

## PLATE 38: Rambler Runabout, 1902

Like so many of the early auto pioneers, Thomas B. Jeffery was first a builder of bicycles. His Rambler automobile, introduced at the Chicago show of 1902, measured seven feet in length, weighed 1500 pounds and listed at $750, f.o.b. Kenosha, Wis. A handsomely styled runabout body finished in Brewster green with red striping gave the car a jaunty air; in front was a bonnet for the storage of clothing and other articles. It was powered by an eight-horsepower, single-cylinder engine with 4½ × 6 inch bore and stroke. The machine could be started with the operator seated in the carriage by means of a crank located at the side. Another novel feature was embodied in the steering arrangement. A horizontal lever, hinged to the vertical shaft, was conveniently located so that either of the passengers could manipulate the carriage. As standard equipment a set of fine-quality wrenches and tools, which would fit every nut and bolt of the carriage, was provided along with an extra set of batteries, one of the latest French pattern horns, a Veeder odometer and a pair of large carriage lamps. The nostalgic name of Rambler was reborn in 1950 when Nash chose to call its new compact line Rambler.

## PLATE 39: Stanley Steamer, 1902

The Stanley Brothers were shrewd Yankee "horse-traders" as well as mechanical wizards. Their first car had appeared in 1897. It was so successful that shortly thereafter Locomobile interests bought their factory and patents for $250,000. In 1902 the Stanleys reentered the steam car field with a redesigned model which rendered the Locomobile almost obsolete. They were now able to buy back their factory and patents for $25,000, one-tenth of what they had sold it for. The 1902 spindle-seated runabout sat on a 72-inch wheelbase chassis with a truss-reinforced rear axle. It weighed about 800 pounds when its 20-gallon water tank and 14-gallon gasoline tank were filled. The car's eight-h.p. engine consisted of two cylinders, had only 13 moving parts and was geared direct to the rear axle. No transmission or gearshift were necessary since the power could be applied as slowly as desired. However, a touch of the throttle lever would accelerate the car instantly. It sold for around $700. One of the more colorful and completely untrue myths which persisted for years held that the Stanley brothers would give you a new car if you could hold their steamer's throttle wide open for three minutes.

## PLATE 40: Studebaker Electric Runabout, 1902

The entry of Studebaker into the automotive field in 1902 with this electric piano-box runabout saw the end of one era and the beginning of another. From a modest start the South Bend, Ind. firm had risen to prominence as one of the world's largest builders of horse-drawn vehicles. Their carriage experience was particularly in evidence in the design of the body of their 1902 runabout. Its angular lines were severely simple yet smart; it was well upholstered with choices of fine-quality leather, cloth or whipcord. Particular care had been taken to provide adequate leg-room and a 28½ inch floor level made for ease of entry or exit. The 24-cell battery was completely enclosed by a neat rear deck. Under the seat the controller was hung, providing speeds of three, six, nine and 13 mph; to the rear of the controller Studebaker placed a 24-ampere, 40-volt Westinghouse motor. An emergency hand brake was provided as well as the regular one operated by foot and, as an added refinement, an indicator which showed exactly the amount of charge remaining in the battery. The $950 purchase price also included: two electric side lamps, a charging plug with 15 feet of cable and a complete tire repair outfit.

## PLATE 41: Winton Touring Car, 1903

On July 26, 1903, 63 days after leaving San Francisco, Dr. Horatio Jackson, his companion, Sewall Crocker, and a stray dog they had picked up enroute, arrived in New York City in a 1903 Winton. This was the first coast-to-coast trip by automobile, a dream which had challenged Americans for many years. The Winton was a stock, two-seated, sport model touring car. Its tonneau had been removed and in its place camping and cooking equipment, an axe, rifle, pistol and a block and tackle rig were stored. In addition to the regular 12-gallon fuel tank under the hood, an extra 20-gallon tank had been installed at the rear. A rugged two-cylinder, 20-h.p. engine powered the machine, and the side kerosene lamps were supplemented by a big acetylene lamp in the front. At the end of Jackson's epic journey the Winton was hardly recognizable as the handsome machine which came from the factory. The Cleveland firm used only fully seasoned ash and poplar, fine hand-buffed leather upholstery, cushioned spring seats stuffed with curled hair and shining laminated wood mudguards. Today visitors to the Smithsonian Institution may see Jackson's Winton—a car which dramatically proved that the automobile could be much more than an expensive toy.

## PLATE 42: Peerless Touring Car, 1903

The Peerless Motor Car Company of Cleveland was another of the many early pioneer firms whose bicycle-making experience led them into the automobile field. By 1903 they had advanced from small motorettes which clearly reflected their bicycle heritage to machines that were world renowned for their performances in hill climbing contests and racing events. The Model "F" 16-h.p. touring car was advertised as being "easily one year ahead of all others." It encompassed many features that gave a good deal of validity to their claim. The car had a French tonneau type body with the motor placed in front under a louvred removable hood. A square, distinctive radiator housed the radiating-tube cooling system. To eliminate problems created by water and gas leakage the two 4½ × 5½" cylinders of the engine had been cast from a single block. Advanced carburetion design, separate Splitdorf coils on each cylinder, an interlocking device to prevent stripping the gears, a McCanna oil pump located at the left of the hood instead of on the dash as was customary with most cars of this period were a few of the features which made the Peerless one of the best engineered autos of 1903.

## PLATE 43: Cadillac Tonneau, 1903

The first Cadillac was completed in March of 1903 by Henry M. Leland. Insisting on absolute precision, he created a car that through the years has remained a synonym for refinement and perfection. The one-cylinder, five-horsepower engine of the 1903 model featured complete interchangeability of parts. It was located in the middle of the chassis and could be readily detached when repairs were necessary. The fact that a safety device was provided, making it impossible to crank the engine with a "too-early" spark, suggests that the necessity of a self-starter was subconsciously in mind. The car had no running boards but patent-leather fenders imparted an air of distinction. A rear-entrance, detachable tonneau could be added to double the runabout's ordinary passenger capacity of two. Cadillac's advertisements for this 1903 model listed some of the following specifications: 72-inch wheelbase, 54½-inch tread, wood artillery wheels, jump spark ignition, 3-inch tires, angle iron frame, rack and gear type steering, total weight of 1360 pounds and price, $850. The latter did not include the heavy kerosene lamps nor a hand-operated bulb horn, which were extra equipment. A cut-off was fitted on the muffler for use on country roads where noise was presumed to be unobjectionable.

## PLATE 44: Ford "A" Tonneau, 1903

On June 16, 1903 a dozen daring stockholders invested $28,000 to form the Ford Motor Company. Their first sale of an automobile, less than a month later, was the beginning of one of the most fabulous industrial developments in the history of motordom. The car was called the Model "A" and appealed to the public immediately. It sold for $950, a price well under most of its competition. In size, it was more compact and it led the market in simplicity. Though not especially fast—30 mph—its ability to withstand the rigors of the rough roads of that period became proverbial. The two-cylinder, 4 × 4 inch, opposed engine was rated at 8 h.p. and cranked from the side. Reporters of the period marvelled at its "simplicity and directness." The car's weight was 1100 pounds, wheelbase 72 inches; 28 × 3 inch tires were used. A two-speed planetary transmission was attached to the engine and a central chain transmitted power to the rear axle. The car stood high above the street; when its tonneau section was removed the rear deck lid could be raised for access to the machinery. Lamps, horn, windshield and top were extra. The latter could be used only when the car had shed its tonneau.

## PLATE 45: Oldsmobile Curved Dash Runabout, 1903

The curved dash Olds in 1901 demonstrated to America that automobiles could be made and sold in quantity. From a figure of 425 in their first year, production zoomed to 5000 by 1904. The mechanical excellence of the car was convincingly established in 1901 when a model was driven from Detroit to New York; in 1903 another curved dash Olds laid claim to being the first light car to make a transcontinental run. The simple 4½-h.p. engine of the 1903 reflected Oldsmobile's philosophy that the greater the number of parts, the more probable breakage. There was one cylinder (4½ × 6"), one piston, one connecting rod and crank, one balance wheel and two valves. The most unforgettable feature of the car was its curved dashboard. Although in general appearance it still resembled a powered buggy, the smoothly rounded dash created an air of elegance which was complemented by the sweeping line of the tiller. The carriage was handsomely finished in rich wine color and black with a high and lasting varnish luster. Light colored striping bordered the edges and the handsome Oldsmobile medallion appeared on each side of the body. Other specifications were: weight, 830 pounds; price $650; tread, 55 inches; wheelbase, 66 inches; water capacity, 5 gallons; gasoline, 4 gallons.

## PLATE 46: Locomobile Tonneau De Luxe, 1904

In its 26 years, from 1903 to 1929, Locomobile produced steam and gasoline cars which are still remembered for their speed, luxury and excellence of design. The 1904 "D" Tonneau De Luxe had been developed by A. L. Riker and was closely fashioned after the German Mercedes Simplex. It sold for $4000 (including extras: five brass lamps, brass horn, tarpaulin, storm apron, tools, 20 spare parts and a tire repair kit). The company aimed its advertising at the wealthy amateur motorist, claiming that their car was the equal of any of the high-priced imported machines. A four-cylinder engine cast in two blocks, with a bore and stroke of 4 × 5″, featuring side exhaust and overhead inlet valves operated by pushrods, powered the Locomobile "D." It was a well-machined and efficient unit, capable of developing 20 h.p. at 2000 r.p.m.'s. Riker had also borrowed from European design for the radiator—a honeycomb type with a fan directly behind it. The 1904 Tonneau De Luxe seated six persons and measured 82 inches at the wheelbase. Locomobile's record in competitive trials progressed steadily until in 1908 it astounded the racing world by winning the international Vanderbilt cup race—a feat never before accomplished by an American car.

## PLATE 47: Rambler Tonneau, 1904

With the introduction of their twin-cylinder models in 1904, Rambler now offered a complete line of eight vehicles, ranging from a small runabout to a medium-sized touring car. The Model "L" was by far the most popular and in it can be seen the designers' realization that along with a mechanically sound

machine they must also give passengers some protection from the weather. A surrey type top, waterproof side curtains and a beveled plate glass windshield provided a degree of comfort not available in the ordinary open car. Though unusually high and somewhat boxy in appearance, the 1904 Rambler Tonneau was still an exceedingly attractive automobile. Its gracefully curving mudguards, the sparkle of well-polished brass lamps (oil on the sides, acetylene gas in the front) and the soft gleam of its rich, buttoned-leather upholstery were pleasing to the eye. A pair of willow wicker baskets, commonly used for picnicking supplies, could be strapped to the sides. Other details of the tonneau: 5 × 6″ two-cylinder engine mounted under the car and rated at 16 h.p.; honeycomb type radiator; weight, 1900 pounds; 30 × 3½″ tires; automatic float feed carburetor; planetary type transmission; 84″ wheelbase, 56½″ tread; speed 6–40 mph; price, $1350, f.o.b. Kenosha, Wis.

## PLATE 48: Studebaker Touring Car, 1904

In the year 1904, the Studebaker Brothers, who had for half a century been famous builders of fine carriages and wagons, sold their first gasoline car to a customer at the gates of their South Bend plant. It was a model 9502, similar to the one shown here. While the engine and chassis were produced by another firm (Garford, of Elyria, Ohio), Studebaker supplied the body. The 9502 was designed for use either as a five-passenger touring car or as a two-passenger runabout (by detaching the tonneau). Studebaker's long tradition of refined craftsmanship was particularly in evidence in the body details. Customers were allowed a choice of either dark green or dark blue, complemented by appropriate striping. Special leather upholstery matched the colors of the body. A bulb horn, two oil side lights and an oil tail lamp were standard equipment. The 1904 Studebaker catalog lists other specifications such as: engine, 2-cylinder horizontal, 16 h.p., 5 × 5½″ bore and stroke; armored wood frame; wheelbase 82″; tread, 56½″; overall length and width, 130 and 69″; lubrication, force feed oiler, sights located on dash; speed, 4–35 mph; price, $1750 including Cape Cart or canopy top. In 1904 Studebaker also produced electric traps, phaetons, stanhopes, runabouts, trucks, etc.

## PLATE 49: Ford "B" Touring Car, 1905

The Ford Model "B" touring car was introduced late in 1904. It represented a move away from the cheaper model Ford had envisioned and was evidently a concession on his part toward the company's directors who wished to capture a greater portion of the high-priced market. The "B" was heavier (1700 pounds), faster (40 mph), bigger (92″ wheelbase) and more expensive ($2000) than anything the company had yet built. A 24-h.p. four-cylinder, copper-jacketed, vertical engine with a 4½ × 5″ bore and stroke was located under the removable hood. Though current for the jump spark ignition was supplied by a storage battery through a vibrator box, the two side lamps were operated by oil. This was the first Ford to be equipped with a reverse gear and it was also the first true touring type body to appear on a Ford. Advertising brochures issued for the "B" stressed the safety features embodied in the simplified control system. There were levers under the steering wheel for the spark and throttle; brake and reverse pedals on the floor, and one big side lever to regulate high and low speeds. If any of these controls were applied in opposition "the only result would be the stopping of the car or the motor."

## PLATE 50: Holsman Surrey, 1905

High wheeler, or auto buggy manufacturers flourished in the first decade of the 20th century when the deeply rutted and muddy country roads made a vehicle with narrow wheels, 3 to 4 feet high, seem quite advantageous. The Holsman Automobile Company of Chicago in offering their 1905 line was able to advance another cogent argument. They maintained that the general construction of their body and chassis was so similar to horse-drawn vehicles that local wheelwrights and wagon shops could make repairs. Their 1905 surrey featured a fringed top on a piano-style buggy body. The rear seat could be removed, allowing ample space to carry grain to the mill or groceries from town. High dished wheels (44″ in front, 48″ in rear) shod with 1⅛″ solid rubber tires were used on this $800 model. All 1905 Holsman cars came with a 10-h.p. air-cooled two-cylinder engine and treads of either 56 or 62 inches. A simple rope-and-pulley transmission engaged bands attached to pulleys on the spokes of the rear wheel to provide speeds of up to 30 mph as well as a reverse. The car's weight totalled 900 pounds and it was set on a tubular frame. Other specifications: jump spark ignition, forced lubrication, 66″ wheelbase.

## PLATE 51: Cadillac "D" Touring Car, 1905

This car reflected many of the changes which were faintly stirring in the automotive world of 1905. Manufacturers were placing more emphasis on larger cars; the French tonneau was being replaced by larger bodies with side doors and speed was deemed secondary to comfort and ease of riding. The four-cylinder Cadillac "D" was an expensive, finely tooled car—the company's first prestige machine. It had a wooden body with 20-inch double side doors at the rear. The front seat was divided and running boards made entry to the car much easier than the small step-plates heretofore used. Leland's insistence on quality can be seen in many other features of the car. He used a five-spring support for the chassis frame, a novel form of flywheel clutch and clutch-releasing mechanism and a newly designed carburetor without float, guaranteed not to be affected by tipping in any direction. The motor was a vertical type, 30 h.p., $4\frac{3}{8} \times 5''$, water-cooled by a centrifugal pump, capable of speeds up to 50 mph. The "D" had a 100-inch wheelbase, weighed 2600 pounds and cost $2800. A test driver of the day enthusiastically described the car as elegant in appearance and "the most highly organized of all automobiles."

## PLATE 52: Stearns "40–45" Limousine, 1906

The F. B. Stearns Company of Cleveland, Ohio is fondly remembered as the producer of some of America's most handsome and luxurious cars for over a quarter of a century (1900–1929). The firm flatly stated that their 1906 machine was "the best automobile" in the world. They claimed that a minimum of 2100 work hours was spent in finishing a car after parts had been received from the foundry. Only one chassis was made in 1906, the 40–45 h.p.; a variety of bodies could be mounted on it. The chauffeur-driven, French-type limousine was made of cast aluminum. It cost $5200 and in deference to the individual tastes of the purchasers, a wide option of colors was permitted. By today's standards the car is exceedingly high. This reflects the design philosophy of the period—that there should be enough room for a person to stand upright in an enclosed car if he wished. Jump-seats in the rear compartment were used to seat additional passengers when necessary. Other specifications: tread and wheelbase, 56 and 118''; 4 cylinders, $4\frac{7}{8} \times 5\frac{1}{8}''$; double side chain drive; weight, 3000 pounds; four forward speeds, one reverse; front tires, $36 \times 4''$, rear, $36 \times 4\frac{1}{2}''$; pressed steel frame and semi-elliptic springs $2\frac{1}{2}''$ wide.

## PLATE 53: Ford "K" Touring Car, 1906

The Model "K" was the largest, most expensive of any of the pre-Model "T" Fords. Almost half of all American cars sold in 1906 fell in the $2275 to $4775 price range and the Ford company believed that the "K" would be their entry to this luxury market. The car was assembled at the Piquette Avenue plant in Detroit. Its six-cylinder, $4\frac{1}{2} \times 4\frac{1}{2}''$ engine was a powerful 40-h.p. vertical type capable of delivering 60 mph. Each of the cylinders was individually cast. Valves, actuated by a single camshaft, were placed on the right side of the motor instead of on the left which was the usual practice. The body was luxurious and could comfortably seat five persons. Flaring rear fenders were joined to the curved ones in the front. A metal running board connected them and provided a place for the acetylene gas tank which lighted the head lamps; oil lamps were located on the side. Like all Ford cars before 1927, the "K" models used a planetary transmission. It had a wheelbase of 114 inches, weighed 2400 pounds and carried a price tag of $2500. After less than a thousand were made, the "K" was discontinued.

## PLATE 54: Autocar Runabout, 1906

1906 was a memorable year for the Autocar Company of Ardmore, Pa. They marketed only two models, a touring car and runabout, but finished the year with an enviable record of successes in hill-climbing contests and reliability runs. 1906 was also the year that the company decided to switch from tiller to wheel steering in their Type X Runabout. The model was proudly advertised as having all control levers assembled at the steering post. "Wheel, gear shift, clutch, throttle and spark control are all within easy reach." It was also claimed that the motor developed "twelve actual horsepower"—a sly dig at manufacturers whose horsepower claims might have been exaggerated. An iron crank case replaced the former aluminum one and the $4 \times 4''$ double-opposed two-cylinder motor was mounted transversely under a French type hood. The frame was of armored wood, hung on $1\frac{1}{2}''$ wide semielliptic four-leaf springs. Particu-

lar care had been taken to make the carrying box at the rear as watertight as possible. Fisk tires of a kind ordinarily found on heavier cars were used on the $28 \times 3''$ sturdy, tubular steel wheels. The car had a short 76-inch wheelbase and weighed only 1370 pounds. Its basic price of $1000 included oil lamps and an extra set of spark plugs.

## PLATE 55: Marmon "D" Touring Car, 1906

The state of Indiana was a prolific producer of fine cars and for a period seemed destined to supplant Detroit as motor capital of the world. The highly regarded Stutz, Auburn, Cord, Duesenberg, Apperson, Elkhart, H.C.S. and many others were all Indiana-made. Nordyke & Marmon set up in Indianapolis in 1876 as milling machinery manufacturers. Their first car was designed by Howard Marmon in 1902; by 1906 the company was able to turn out a machine which finished the 1200-mile Glidden Tour with a perfect score. The Model "D" touring body was made of cast aluminum and featured a novel V-4 engine, advertised as "a mechanical masterpiece." Its $4\frac{5}{8} \times 4\frac{1}{2}''$ cylinders were set at 90° to each other with cooling being done by circular flanges. Another engineering feat centered around an unusual, patented, double three-point suspension system. This construction was supposed to free the frame from strain when one of the wheels was raised from the ground by any obstruction. The tonneau of the "D" was 50 inches inside and could comfortably seat 3 persons. Weighing 2400 pounds, it listed at $3000. This price included such extras as a pair of acetylene gas lamps in the front, a bulb horn, a pump and a tire repair kit.

## PLATE 56: Packard "S-24" Victoria, 1906

By 1906 a number of Packard design features had emerged which were to become synonymous with the car. Several of these are apparent on the "24" touring model (officially designated as the "S"). The indented hexagon on the hub can be seen. This was intended as a place to insert a tool for removing the hub. Another distinctive mark of Packard is observable in the yoke-shaped radiator design. The 1906 Packard "24" was a luxurious yet rugged machine, equally suited for extended cross-country touring or short runs about town. It listed at $4000 and six other body styles were offered that year with prices ranging up to $5225 for a landaulet model. A hinged foot-rail was provided in the tonneau of the touring car as well as storage room under the rear seat and in a removable locker at the rear of the front seat. One writer who accompanied the Packard "24" on a demonstration run said that it glided smoothly on city streets, danced in and out of heavy traffic like a light-weight and on an open, hilly stretch, reached 55 mph. Some of its principal specifications were: $4\frac{1}{2} \times 5\frac{1}{2}''$ four-cylinder engine; 119'' wheelbase; weight, 2800 pounds; sliding gear transmission; three forward speeds, one reverse.

## PLATE 57: Cadillac "M" Touring Car, 1906

In Cadillac's 1906 Model "M" light touring car, the designers created a body that is still regarded as a classic in styling. They used the traditional graceful curves usually found in a Victoria coach. The forward sweep, repeated on the front and the rear compartments of the tonneau, formed a delightful pattern; it was widely copied and came to be known as a "tulip type" style. The gay finish of the car was also striking—purple lake (a deep, rich wine color) body panels and doors with light carmine striping, dark carmine chassis. Buff or red buttoned upholstery was supplied and for an extra $75 the purchaser could have a dark-colored Cape Cart top which, when raised, was secured to the frame at the front of the car by two leather straps. It was powered by the same one-cylinder, $5 \times 5''$ engine which Cadillac had used since 1902. This was a reliable two-cycle, 10-h.p. motor mounted under the body. While the car's wheelbase measured 76 inches, a wheel tread size of either 56 or 61 inches was available. It was relatively light at 1350 pounds as well as relatively inexpensive, costing $950. A planetary transmission, jump spark ignition, chain drive and a rack and pinion steering system were features of the car.

## PLATE 58: Maxwell Tourabout, 1907

There is little doubt that Maxwell was among the best of the early small cars. It was well made, a good performer within its limited range, simple in its mechanical details and outstandingly reliable. Maxwells were first manufactured in Tarrytown, N.Y. in 1904. Commencing with 1913, operations were moved to Detroit and in 1925 the Maxwell name was dropped, to emerge a year later as the Chrysler "50." In 1907 the Maxwell company proudly announced that their Tourabout Model "RL" incorporated no fundamental changes. Its distinguishing features—thermo-syphon water circulation, unit construction of the engine and transmission, three-point suspension of the motor and pressed steel bodies—had already been in use since 1904. The makers installed a two-cylinder, $4\frac{1}{2} \times 4''$ engine under the hood. This was capable of driving the 1150-pound car at speeds up to 35 mph. The gear shift lever was located on the right, a feature common at the time. However, unlike the usual practice, the shift lever was in high gear position when pulled all the way up. This was a safety factor intended to lessen the need for stooping. The Tourabout had a 72-inch wheelbase and carried sufficient fuel, water and oil for a 100-mile run.

## PLATE 59: Apperson Touring Car, 1907

In 1907, Apperson Brothers of Kokomo, Ind. declared that it would build exactly "100 cars each year, no more, no less." Each would be a "model of perfection" and following the company's long-standing policy, every one would be thoroughly road-tested before release to the public. Their 1907 models ranged from the low-slung, racy "Jack Rabbit" capable of 75 mph to this luxurious and uniquely styled touring car. Its body, specially made by Kimball of Chicago, displayed several unusual design techniques. Gay vertical striping formed a novel pattern on the rear compartment and the front was highlighted by an interesting use of closely woven canework. Fifteen to eighteen coats of paint, then two coats of rubbing varnish and a final finishing coat were applied to each body. With the special attention required for each car it is not difficult to understand why Apperson charged $4000 ($4200 with cape top) for a touring model of this kind. The 40-h.p., $5 \times 5''$ engine was equipped with two jump spark plugs on each of its four cylinders. One plug was supplied with current from the magneto; the other, by storage battery. The 1907 touring car weighed almost 3000 pounds, had a wheelbase of 114 inches and was driven by double side chains.

## PLATE 60: Buick "G" Runabout, 1907

The 1907 Buick Model "G" was not as large nor as powerful as many rival makes on the market that year yet it enjoyed great popularity and a large measure of commercial success. Buick advertised that exactly 535 of these turtleback runabouts were made and "every one of them sold." They were simply constructed, easy to operate and widely regarded as cars that were equally at home on the treacherous dirt roads of the country or cobblestone streets of the city. At a time when many makers were moving their motors to the front of the car, Buick still hung the "G's" engine under the driver's seat. It cranked from the side and transmitted power to the rear axle by a chain drive. Foot pedals operated the clutch, brakes and reverse gear; spark and throttle device were within fingertip reach under the steering wheel. Buick maintained that their internal expanding hub brake would positively hold on any hill the car could climb. With a 2-cylinder $4\frac{1}{2} \times 5''$ engine, 89'' wheelbase, a weight of 1800 pounds, five brass lamps and a shiny bulb horn, the "G" runabout was truly a bargain in its day at $1150. International tires measuring $30 \times 3\frac{1}{2}''$ came with the car.

## PLATE 61: Pope-Waverley "60-A" Surrey, 1907

Colonel Albert A. Pope, a former bicycle manufacturer, was one of the earliest car-makers to grasp the concept of trying to offer a varied line of automobiles to the public. Every segment of the market, from the low price field to the luxury range, was blanketed by his Pope-Toledo, Pope-Tribune and Pope-Hartford gasoline cars. For those who might prefer electrics, he could offer this Pope-Waverley made in Indianapolis. The surrey was a handsome machine which well illustrates what a really short step the electric vehicle was from the horse-drawn carriage in 1907. It cost $1825 and could be had with either the fringed canopy top or a full leather extension type. Two motors of three h.p. each were suspended rigidly to the rear axle. Current obtained from the 42-cell Exide or National battery made possible speeds of up to 15 mph. Front electric lights, a continuous running board and fender and an electric warning bell (operated by a push button located in the side steering lever) were a few of the Pope-Waverley's refinements. Other specifications: weight, 2680 pounds;

wheelbase, 90''; tires, $30 \times 3\frac{1}{2}''$ front, $30 \times 4''$ rear. The company's advertising stressed that in starting the car "no fuel, grease, water, physical exertion, soiled hands or violent expressions" were necessary.

## PLATE 62: Cadillac "H" Limousine, 1907

Leland's passion for precision of machined parts reached further heights in 1907 when he imported into the U.S.A. the first set of Johansson gauge blocks from Sweden. The next year three Cadillacs were shipped to England, disassembled and parts completely scrambled. Two mechanics armed with only wrenches and screwdrivers reassembled the parts and the three Cadillacs drove off on a 500-mile run. This convincing proof of complete interchangeability of parts gained for Cadillac the first Dewar trophy ever given an American firm. The "H" limousine was an outstanding example of Cadillac quality. Its rear compartment was luxuriously upholstered in rich black leather over deep coiled springs and genuine curled hair. A speaking tube provided communication with the chauffeur who sat protected from the elements by a top and a windshield. Cut-glass oil lamps at the side added a touch of elegance. A long 102-inch wheelbase and sturdy four-leaf springs of the finest steel available, imparted a ride which for the time was the epitome of ease and comfort. Only specially selected second growth hickory was used in the artillery-type wheels. These carried large $34 \times 4\frac{1}{2}''$ tires on Midgely Universal rims. The limousine cost $3600 and its almost 3000 pounds were driven by a 30-h.p., four-cylinder motor.

## PLATE 63: Oldsmobile "A" Touring Car, 1907

An impressive showing in the 1906 Glidden Tour encouraged Oldsmobile to continue its recently introduced Palace Touring Car model; in 1907 it was known as the "A." This car was one of the first American makes to furnish an enclosure for the front-seat passenger and driver. The small front doors were tastefully upholstered in leather and the one on the left swung forward to allow entry for passenger and driver. A well-designed luggage carrier was placed at the rear of the car; in front unusually high fenders almost paralleled the radiator line. Oldsmobile's parade of 1907 models included, in addition to the four-cylinder "A," the familiar, single-cylinder curved dash runabout. (If desired, it now could be ordered with a straight or "piano-box" front.) The company, however, pinned its hopes on the "A" and expected to sell about 900 of the touring cars at the price of $2750 each. Some of its main specifications were: $4\frac{1}{2} \times 4\frac{3}{4}''$ four-cylinder engine of 35-40 h.p.; three speeds forward, one reverse; wheelbase, $106\frac{1}{2}''$; weight 2600 pounds; tires, $34 \times 3\frac{1}{2}''$ front and $34 \times 4''$ rear; jump spark ignition with two sets of batteries; sliding gear transmission; Timken rear axles with gear ratio of approximately 3:1.

## PLATE 64: S. & M. Simplex Limousine, 1907

The Simplex automobile of 1907 bears the curious distinction of a car that has had two names. It began the year as the "S. & M. Simplex" and ended as just plain "Simplex." Smith & Mabley, Inc. of New York City were early casualties of the 1907 business panic. The car they made, however, was continued by another firm whose goal was also to build a machine that was every bit as good as the finest European cars of the time. Two chassis were offered by Simplex in 1907; one was a 30-h.p. 106'' wheelbase model; the other was the 50-h.p. model, shown here, with a 124'' wheelbase. Both were made of the finest chrome-nickel steel available, "Krupp E. F. 60" imported from Essen, Germany. A great variety of bodies, from America's most respected custom-body houses, were available for mounting on the Simplex chassis. Seven-passenger limousines listed at $7000 and up. The 50 h.p. engine was a four-cylinder, four-cycle, T-head type with bore and stroke of $5\frac{3}{4} \times 5\frac{3}{4}''$. It gave an immense piston displacement of 597 cubic inches. The weight of the chassis alone was 2600 pounds; with the body, around 3400 pounds. Imported continental tires, baggage rack, robe rack and foot rest were standard equipment on the limousine.

## PLATE 65: Pierce Great Arrow Touring Car, 1908

Among antique and classic car fanciers, the famous triumvirate of Packard, Peerless and Pierce-Arrow is regarded with awe. Their cars are the prized possession today of a fortunate few. Pierce-Arrow's epitaph, written in 1938 by a national magazine, unkindly but succinctly read "Bird Cages to Bankruptcy." George N. Pierce started in 1865 as a builder of bird cages, ice boxes and other household items; he graduated to bicycles and in 1901, to motor cars. Almost from the beginning, Pierce believed that the kind of car he wished to build could not be mass-produced but must be tastefully and carefully made for the upper-class buyer. His decision to concentrate on mechanical excellence bore fruit as the Pierce-Arrow won the first four Glidden Tours (1904–1907). This six-cylinder 1907 touring model was as fine a machine as materials and techniques of the day could produce. It had a 40-h.p., precision-made engine of 4¼ × 4¾" that was almost perfectly balanced. The seven-passenger touring body sat on a huge 130-inch wheelbase chassis and carried a 20-gallon gasoline tank under the front seat. About seven to eight miles per gallon was average mileage for cars of this size. Pierce priced the car at $5500, f.o.b. Buffalo, N. Y.

## PLATE 66: Rauch & Lang Brougham, 1908

The graceful and luxurious living of a bygone era is aptly symbolized by this quiet and sedate electric carriage. Between 1896 and 1928 at least 54 makes of electric cars were offered for sale to the American public. The last survivor, the Detroit Electric, held out until almost the beginning of World War II. Of the estimated 50,000 electric carriages made in America, almost 14,000 were produced by Rauch and Lang of Cleveland. Their advertising for the company's 1908 line proudly pointed out that they had been building fine vehicles for a select patronage since 1853. Three separate chassis with bodies ranging from small, open stanhopes to this large chauffeur-driven brougham were available. Unlike most of the other body styles, the brougham featured a steering wheel instead of a tiller. Its rear compartment with cut-glass flower vases, rich upholstery, toilet cases and spacious windows was elegantly appointed. It had an irresistible appeal to those who placed an accent on luxury and comfort rather than speed. The 1908 Brougham weighed 3600 pounds, cost $3800 and came on a 103-inch wheelbase. It was chain-driven, drawing current from 15 batteries of 24 cells each. The car could attain speeds up to 18 mph.

## PLATE 67: Stanley Roadster, 1908

In 1908 only four steam cars were exhibited at the New York Auto Show and it seemed just a matter of time before these would succumb to the gasoline age. The magic name of Stanley, however, was a long time dying. Its reflection of the Stanley Brothers' genius enabled it to survive until 1927. Car buyers in 1908 were still talking about the world's record a Stanley Steamer had recently set at Ormond Beach, Florida. Fred Marriott in 1906 had sped across a five-mile course in a Stanley at the amazing speed of 127 mph. The 1908 models were equipped with a boiler and an engine exactly like the Ormond Beach car, except that power had been scaled down by one-half. This model, the "H-5," was designated as the "Gentlemen's Speedy Roadster." It carried the 26 × 14" boiler as well as the burner under its rounded hood; a 13-gallon gasoline tank was placed at the rear. Wheelbase and tread measurements were 100 and 54 inches and the car was driven by a 20-h.p., 3⅝ × 5" engine. Stanley Bros. priced it at $1350. Their advertising stated that the Gentlemen's Roadster was "intended for those who wished to hit up to a speed of 65 or 70 miles per hour on a good, safe road."

## PLATE 68: Ford Model "T" Touring Car, 1909

In October 1908 the first of 15 million Model T's that were to be built took to the road. By the time production had ceased in 1927, the Ford "T" had brought fame and fortune to its maker and had easily become the most famous car in the world. It was a high, somewhat drab, ungraceful-looking car, neither stylish nor pretty. Yet it had the redeeming qualities of lightness and simplicity of construction; it was easy to repair and spare parts could be obtained in any hamlet in the country. The entire power-plant and transmission of the 1909 Ford were completely enclosed in one case. The 20-h.p. engine's four cylinders of 3¾ × 4" were cast in one solid block which was covered by a detachable cylinder head. Dry batteries of the earlier cars had been replaced by a magneto built into the flywheel. Now, the company declared "every time the flywheel revolves you get a series of sparks." The car measured 100 inches at the wheelbase, weighed 1200 pounds and cost $850. To give it greater flexibility on rough roads, three-point suspension was featured throughout. Ford claimed that the semielliptical transverse springs were accident-proof and almost impossible to break. Coupés, roadsters, landaulets and town cars were also part of the 1909 Ford line.

## PLATE 69: Studebaker "A" Suburban, 1909

By 1908 Studebaker's sales had climbed to all-time heights and the company's principal problem centered around building enough cars to meet demands. The solution was simple; it lay in acquiring the exclusive marketing rights to the entire output of the Detroit-made E-M-F auto. Thus, Studebaker dealers in 1909 were able to show a variety of 17 different models in all. The Studebaker "A" Suburban was boomed as being the answer to motorists who wished a rig that was a happy medium between the runabout and the touring car. It was, their advertising claimed, "adaptable." As the needs of the moment required, it could alternately become a smart runabout, a light four-passenger touring car or a combination passenger and luggage car. A large storage area lay under the removable rear seat and, behind it, a luggage hamper. The body was essentially an adaptation of the type of body used on light wagons and heavy road buggies. It rested on a short 104-inch wheelbase chassis and was driven by a four-cylinder, 30-h.p. 4⅛ × 5¼" engine. The low, racy appearance of the Suburban was enhanced by its sporty-looking cowl. Studebaker priced it at $3500 and included an extra rumble seat, five lamps, horn and tools.

## PLATE 70: Knox "M" Limousine, 1909

The 1909 Knox featured both air-cooled and water-cooled engines, three different-sized chassis and a large selection of interesting body styles. There were touring cars, landaulets, single and double rumble sportabouts, tonneauettes, raceabouts and dignified limousines of the type shown here. The body was placed on the 48-h.p. model "M" chassis. It was constructed of wood and metal and seated five passengers in the rear compartment. Only fine quality material was used in the car's upholstery—hand-buffed leather, whipcord, imported goatskin and broadcloth. For $6000 the company included mirror lens headlights, square oil lamps on the side, a speaking tube, storm curtains for the front seat and an extra rim to carry the spare tire. A double ignition system was used. Spark plugs on the right side of the motor were supplied current from a gear-driven high-tension magneto. The plugs on the left were wired for current generated by a battery and Connecticut coil and timer. The Knox was a product of Springfield, Mass. Some of the brougham's other specifications were: 127" wheelbase; 5½ × 5½" bore and stroke; water-cooled; weight, 3600 pounds; selective sliding gear transmission with four forward speeds, one reverse; 36 × 4½" tires; double side chain drive.

## PLATE 71: Thomas Flyer Touring Car, 1909

Man's imagination was truly ignited in 1908 by the remarkable feat of a stock six-cylinder Thomas Flyer car. In a globe-girdling race from New York to Paris, it had triumphed over the most rigorous tests conceivable. By crossing the finish line well ahead of the five other formidable entries—all from Europe—it proved conclusively that America could produce automobiles that were equal to any in the world. The E. R. Thomas Company of Buffalo, N. Y. now offered in their new 1909 Model "K" six-cylinder touring car, the same rugged construction that characterized the prize-winning Flyer. The powerful 70-h.p. engine featured inlet and exhaust valves on opposite sides of the cylinders, an extra-large crank case and a cast steel flywheel with integral external fan blades. Sheet aluminum was used in the body and for $6000 the purchaser received a folding windshield, a luggage rack in the rear and foot pedals with adjustable ends to suit the needs of the individual driver. The touring car's wheelbase measured 140 inches. With its powerful engine, its handsome body and its prestige as a car that had won the New York to Paris Race, the 1909 Thomas caused wealthy American motorists to consider carefully before turning to Europe for their cars.

## PLATE 72: Hudson Roadster, 1910

Detroit was slowly edging into its title as the "Motor City" of the world by the beginning of 1910. Of the 290 different American vehicles produced in 1909, 25 came from Detroit. One of the most promising was made by the Hudson Motor Car Company. Their first car rolled out of the factory on July 3, 1909 and was an instantaneous success. The motoring public seemed to agree that it was, as advertised, "a good car at a low price." This 1910 roadster carried a price tag of $1000 and was the companion model to the $1150 touring car. It had a mahogany dash, graceful fenders curving well down over the wheels and a small aluminum step plate. The body was secured to the chassis by four large bolts and rubber shims; the latter did wonders to lessen the squeaks ordinarily found in cars of the period. Artillery wheels (10 spokes in front, 12 in rear) of good-grade hickory carried clincher rims for 32 × 3½″ tires. If the owner wished, he could mount a large 25-gallon gas tank in the rear instead of the rumble seat. The weight of the roadster was 1800 pounds, wheelbase 100 inches. It was powered by a 20–25 h.p., four-cylinder, 3¾ × 4½″ engine.

## PLATE 73: Chalmers-Detroit Coupé, 1910

Hugh Chalmers was a super-salesman, one of the most outstanding of the early auto industry. In 1908 he was persuaded to switch from selling cash registers to cars. The principal inducement had been an interest in the Thomas-Detroit company, whose name, and the name of whose car, was to be changed to Chalmers-Detroit. Chalmers quickly placed advertising and sales on a national basis, entered his cars in numerous hill climbs, road races and special tours. One of the company's shrewdest publicity campaigns culminated in the award of a 1910 Chalmers-Detroit to the winner of the American League batting championship, Ty Cobb. In addition to being well advertised, the 1910 Chalmers-Detroit was also an excellently designed, mechanically sound machine. The smart, inside-drive coupé became a very popular model. It was fully convertible and could be turned into a roadster "in a few minutes" by removing the body and substituting roadster seats. The latter were included along with Bosch magneto, gas lamps, Prest-O-Lite tank and four-inch tires for $2100. Other specifications: wheelbase, 115 inches; engine, 30 h.p., four-cylinder, 4 × 4½″; float feed carburetor; three-speed transmission; bevel gear drive; worm and gear type steering gear.

## PLATE 74: Reo Roadster, 1910

Ransom E. Olds is one of the two American car makers who had the honor of having not one, but two well-known automobiles named after him. (The other was H. C. Stutz.) Olds withdrew from the Oldsmobile organization in 1904 and joined a Lansing firm about to produce the Reo car. The company had long been a consistent exponent of the two-cylinder engine. Their announcement in late 1909 that a four-cylinder Reo would soon be marketed was greeted with interest. Though this model "S" four-cylinder roadster was the star attraction for Reo buyers in 1910, the company still offered a two-cylinder model as well as the dependable, unchanged, one-cylinder runabout. The four-cylinder engine had vertical cylinders cast in pairs, 4 × 4½″ bore and stroke, and a horsepower rating of 30–35. It followed the growing tendency of designers toward a relatively long stroke. Another change which was occurring can be seen in the placement of the steering wheel and controls on the left side rather than the right. Automotive writers of 1910 described the car as "fast, racy looking" and believed that its large 34 × 3½″ wheels and long 108″ wheelbase would result in "very comfortable riding qualities." The Roadster weighed 2100 pounds; its cost, $1250.

## PLATE 75: Buick "10" Toy Tonneau, 1910

The Buick model "10" was introduced in 1908, the same year Buick Motor Company became the cornerstone of the newly formed General Motors organization. By 1910 the model had proven to be Buick's "bread and butter" car. Though its remarkable successes in road and stock races were well publicized, the company still aimed part of its advertising at the fair sex with the claim that it was "the most popular car in the world for women." The toy tonneau body of the 1910 Buick appears to be almost as large as most of the standard-sized tonneaus of the day. Its wheelbase, however, was a short 92 inches and only four passengers could be accommodated. The valve-in-head engine, a Buick trademark since 1904, was still being used. The 1910 motor was a four-cylinder affair with bore and stroke of 3¾ × 3¾″ and a rating of 18 h.p. A planetary transmission provided only two speeds forward and one reverse. Other specifications show that the car was water-cooled and shaft-driven. It came equipped with a cone clutch, jump spark ignition, 30 × 3½″ tires, Remy magneto, Schebler carburetor and pressed steel frame, and cost $1150 f.o.b. Flint. More than 11,000 "10's" were produced by Buick in 1910.

## PLATE 76: Packard Berline, 1910

The clientele of the Packard Motor Car Company included some of the most discriminating purchasers in the U.S. In the 1910 berline model they were offered a vehicle combining practicality with richness and individuality. It was

a large, completely enclosed seven-passenger limousine type with a movable window behind the driver. As with most berlines, Packard's was more sumptuously fitted and bigger than the ordinary limousine. Perhaps the most interesting feature was the use of shaped glass windows. This produced a pleasing effect when contrasted with the angular lines ordinarily found in 1910 cars, but also created a problem since the shaped glass was hard to replace. As befitted a machine costing over $6000, Packard placed the berline on their largest and most powerful chassis—the "30" with a wheelbase of 123½ inches. A four-cylinder, 30-h.p. engine of 5 × 5½ inches powered the car and was lubricated by a splash-type system. Two drip sight feeds on the dashboard indicated oil levels at all times. One of the driver's chores with the approach of darkness was to light the acetylene gas head lights. To do this he had to get out of his car, open the lamp door, strike a match, turn on the gas and adjust the flame.

## PLATE 77: Sears Motor Buggy, 1910

On two different occasions in its long history, Sears, Roebuck and Company of Chicago, Ill. included automobiles among the many thousands of products it handled. The Allstate was briefly sold by the company from 1952–53. Much earlier, however, in the years 1908 to 1912, the mail-order house marketed a trim, high-wheeled motor buggy under the name of Sears. All orders were on a cash basis and the car was shipped to the purchaser in a crate along with explicit directions for assembling. The 1910 Sears is representative of a particularly unique American automotive development—the high wheeler. These vehicles enjoyed about a decade of popularity and were especially in demand in Midwest rural areas where unimproved roads were the rule. They were characterized by wheels of three to four feet in diameter, a high ground clearance, light weight, small economical engines and buggy type piano-box bodies. The Sears model "L" shown here sold at $495, weighed 1000 pounds and steered by a side lever. Its wheelbase was short, only 72 inches. An air-cooled, 14-h.p., two-cylinder double opposed engine of 4⅛ × 4″ produced speeds up to 25 mph. While the "L" was fitted with pneumatic tires, the four other 1910 Sears models came with uninflated hard rubber tires.

## PLATE 78: Oakland "K" Touring Car, 1910

The 40-horsepower Oakland automobile is regarded with good reason as one of "The cars that built GM." In 1910 the company priced its "K" touring model at $1700 and the public was quick to realize that at this price the Oakland was indeed a bargain. The car was neatly styled and roomy. It boasted numerous successes in hill-climbing contests and carried the prestige of having been designed by one of America's foremost automotive designers, Alanson P. Brush. Clean straight lines characterized his styling approach. The car's beautifully finished mahogany dash was bound in heavy brass moulding. Linoleum-covered floor boards, aluminum doors, heavily tufted fine grade leather upholstery and a gasoline tank with a two-gallon reserve were a few other notable features incorporated into the 1910 Oakland. Its power plant was a lively four-cylinder, four-cycle, vertical engine with 4½-inch bore and 5-inch stroke. The engine was water-cooled with the cooling being assisted by a fan built into the flywheel. Oakland claimed a top speed of 60 mph for its "40" models. Other specifications: weight, 2250 pounds; wheelbase, 112 inches; controls, hand throttle and spark, foot pedal brake and accelerator with emergency brake lever; lubrication, force feed and splash.

## PLATE 79: Brewster Limousine, 1911

No finer exponents of the craft of custom body building can be found among American firms than Brewster & Company of New York City. Their long history covered a span of about 124 years; 95 of these, starting in 1810, were devoted to horse-drawn vehicles. In addition to building bodies for other cars, Brewster marketed an automobile under its own name from 1915 to 1925. The company's enviable reputation, however, sprang from works of art such as this limousine body specially created for an individual buyer and mounted on a 1911 French Delaunay-Belleville chassis. Brewster's order forms went so far as to provide for the size of the purchaser and his chauffeur, upholstery, interior woodwork, etc. A choice was even available in the seat springs—hard, medium or soft. The chassis on which Brewster fitted this handsome body measured 138 inches at the wheelbase and carried a six-cylinder, 25-h.p. engine. It also featured acetylene gas head lamps, jump spark ignition and a selective sliding gear transmission with four forward speeds and one reverse.

The rounded radiator was a proud trademark of Delaunay-Belleville for many years. With a price tag of $7750 the Brewster limousine was one of 1911's most expensive and exclusive cars.

## PLATE 80: Alco Touring Car, 1911

It is regrettable that the builders of this powerful, well-made car found it necessary to suspend automotive production in 1913. The American Locomotive Company's automobile was at one time considered America's answer to the legendary Rolls-Royce of England. With factories in Providence, R.I., the company first built the French Berliet on a royalty basis. In late 1908 their super-ultra Alco, backed by assets of $50,000,000, was placed on the market. Success in the racing circuits followed almost immediately; in 1909, and again in 1910, a six-cylinder stripped Alco touring model defeated all comers in the famed Vanderbilt Cup Race. Along with their 1911 catalog, the company sent a letter advising that if a suitable type of body was not found in the circular, to let them know; that "we will be glad to supply about any style you may wish." The handsome 60-h.p. touring car was certainly one of the more impressive of their standard line. Its heavy, reinforced chassis of special steel measured 134 inches at the wheelbase and was five inches wide at certain points. An equally sturdy, six-cylinder, 60-h.p. motor of $4\frac{3}{4} \times 5\frac{1}{2}''$ powered the car. Alco's touring model weighed 4125 pounds with top, tools, trunk rack and other equipment; its price, $6000.

## PLATE 81: Buick "26" Runabout, 1911

With production figures of around 30,000 cars for 1910, Buick felt that there was little to be gained by making any but minor changes in the 1911 line. Their car was by this time a well-refined, practical machine developed to the point where fairly extensive journeys might be undertaken with confidence. It still required cranking, tires were a constant worry and parts were often difficult to obtain. Yet the 1911 Buick represented an amazing advance in style, comfort and mechanical ability over its forerunners of only a few short years ago. The "26" runabout for 1911 had neat metal fore doors in front and a 25-gallon gasoline tank in the rear. Behind the tank there was space "for a dress suit case or small trunk." The high rear fenders afforded an especially good view of the full elliptic rear springs with scroll ends. Right-hand steering was still employed by Buick, and within easy reach of the driver were levers for emergency braking and gear changes. The runabout's dash was three-ply veneer, walnut finish, and its running boards and front floor boards were covered with linoleum and bound in brass. The car featured a $4 \times 4''$ four-cylinder, valve-in-head engine, had a 100-inch wheelbase and cost $1050.

## PLATE 82: White "30" Landaulet, 1911

The White company's colorful career in the automotive arena began in 1901. Long a manufacturer of quality sewing machines, the Cleveland firm marketed a steam car that year and soon added a companion line of gasoline vehicles. By 1911 they were turning out luxurious equipages in the town-car line—limousines, landaulets and coupés. The 1911 landaulet model was excellently appointed and carried a price tag of $3800. It was mounted on a sturdy, chrome-nickel steel frame and powered by a dependable four-cylinder, 30-h.p. long-stroke engine of $3\frac{3}{4}'' \times 5\frac{1}{8}''$ bore and stroke. Cars of this type were designed primarily for town service where streets were relatively smooth. White tried to insure a comfortable ride by installing large semielliptic springs measuring 42 inches in the front, $48\frac{1}{2}$ in the rear. The "GB" landaulet shown here featured a selective sliding type transmission with four forward speeds and one reverse, a leather-faced cone clutch and an aluminum-alloy crank case. White's 1911 catalog listed numerous refinements which they believed would appeal to women: silk curtains to shade the French plate windows, electric dome lights, polished rosewood window sashes and a choice of broadcloth, whipcord or leather upholstery in any shade desired.

## PLATE 83: Matheson Toy Tonneau, 1911

It has been adjudged that no product of industry ever improved so rapidly as the American motor car. A major share of the credit for this improvement must be laid to the strenuous competition the automobile encountered in early-day races, hill climbs, reliability runs and endurance contests. Matheson's

successes were abundant. They led the Wilkes-Barre, Pa. company to guarantee sweepingly in 1911 that their Silent Six was "better constructed, swifter, more economical in fuel consumption and tire wear, more comfortable . . . than any other six-cylinder car on the market." While the toy tonneau model may not have lived up to all these glowing claims, it was a remarkably well-made, handsome machine. The $4\frac{1}{2} \times 5''$ engine was a 50-h.p. valve-in-head type with cylinders cast in pairs. These cylinders were water-jacketed for cooling and featured a $\frac{3}{4}$ inch offset. A multiple-disc clutch was employed along with a dual-ignition system (Bosch magneto and battery), semielliptic springs in front, scroll elliptic in the rear and a constant-level splash system of lubrication. The Silent Six was shaft-driven, cost $3500 and had a wheelbase of $125\frac{1}{2}$ inches. Toy tonneaus came in either deep blue with black leather, cream with green leather or "special colors to order."

## PLATE 84: Mercer Raceabout, 1911

The Mercer Raceabout is one of the most sought-after of all American antique cars. Auto historians estimate that about 500 Raceabouts were built from 1910 to 1915; only a handful survive today. The car was a true sports type in every sense. It was, first of all, strictly functional with no frills or unnecessary extras. In general layout it closely followed the pattern of the racing cars of the day—a long hood enclosing a powerful engine, a couple of open bucket seats, a large gasoline tank behind the driver and several spare tires strapped to the rear. Mercer's reputation for speed became legendary as the car won race after race throughout the country. The Raceabout was guaranteed to do 70 mph; however, in May, 1912 at Santa Monica, California, Ralph De Palma drove one at an average speed of 80 mph over a 20-mile course. Though the car was offered in three different color options, Canary Yellow seemed to be the favorite and in time became a Mercer Raceabout trademark. Other specifications for 1911 were: engine, 30-h.p., four-cylinder, T-Head, overhead-valve type with $4\frac{3}{8} \times 5''$ bore and stroke; weight, 2300 pounds; wheelbase, 108 inches; tires, $32 \times 4$ inches; price $2500, f.o.b. Trenton, N.J.

## PLATE 85: Rambler Landaulet, 1911

The quiet dignity of the landaulet body style is charmingly exemplified by the smart 1911 Rambler shown in this illustration. It was handsomely upholstered in blue broadcloth and its convertible top could be easily lowered in fair weather. An adjustable footrail, polished mahogany door and window sashes and an electric cigar lighter were only a few of its luxurious appointments. A total of five passengers could be seated in the rear compartment through the use of two drop seats. Rambler placed their landaulet on a 120-inch wheelbase chassis and used a four-cylinder, $5 \times 5\frac{1}{2}''$, 45-horsepower engine in this model. While its tires were fairly large at $37 \times 5''$, even larger ones of $41 \times 5''$ could be had on some of the other Rambler cars for 1911. Big eight-inch gas headlights mounted at a height designed to give superior lighting, combination oil and electric side lights and a spare wheel and tire mounted in the fender well were included in the laundaulet's price of $3650. One reassuring note about the safety of their product was pointed out in Rambler's 1911 catalog: "Each car is required in test to come to a full stop within 50 feet at 18 mph." The Kenosha, Wisconsin firm produced a total of 3000 units in 1911.

## PLATE 86: Simplex Speedster, 1912

This 1912 speedster is undoubtedly the world's best known Simplex automobile, having been viewed over the years by an estimated 60 million visitors to the Smithsonian Institution. Its low, racy lines and no-nonsense, lean look hint at the explosive power packed under the hood—power which made it the darling of early speed devotees. The car was chain-driven with a 50-h.p., four-cylinder, T-Head motor of $5\frac{3}{4} \times 5\frac{3}{4}''$ bore and stroke; speeds of 80 mph and up were common. Aluminum was used for the crankcase and each cylinder had an intake valve on the right side and an exhaust valve on the left; both were operated by their respective camshafts. Another interesting feature centered around the cooling system. Instead of a fan behind the radiator, Simplex utilized flywheel spokes to act as a suction fan. Louvres were omitted from the hood to help the flywheel fan operate more efficiently. Large semi-elliptic springs were placed at each wheel and braking was accomplished by internal-expanding shoes on the rear-wheel drums. Acetylene self-starters, bulb horns and Dietz combination electric-kerosene sidelights were standard equipment. A siren was also provided. Despite a price tag of around $6000, the entire 1912 Simplex output was spoken for a year in advance.

## PLATE 87: Abbott-Detroit "30" Roadster, 1912

Early-day roadsters admittedly sacrificed the room and weather protection found in touring and enclosed cars for other advantages. They were easy to drive; easy to handle in crowded traffic; fast on the hills and bad roads; a car with particular appeal to the professional or business man who travelled extensively. Abbott-Detroit's 1912 fore-door roadster was well designed and adequately powered to meet these requirements. It boasted a rugged 30-horsepower engine with four cylinders of 4⅛" × 4¼" bore and stroke as well as an almost indestructible pressed-steel channel section frame. The roadster sold for $1275 less top, windshield and speedometer; for another $100 the dealer would include those three items. The electric self-starter was just beginning to appear around this time and Abbott-Detroit was quick to join the parade by offering one as optional equipment ($50) in 1912. In keeping with the car's slogan "Built for permanence," its makers furnished a guarantee on each car "for its entire life." Some of the specifications for the roadster were: wheelbase, 110 inches; ignition, Splitdorf dual system, with dry cells for starting; water-cooled, circulation by gear-driven centrifugal pump; worm type, semireversible steering gear; three-ply, black walnut veneer dashboard.

## PLATE 88: Packard "30" Close-Coupled, 1912

Packard's big news for 1912 was the introduction of a six-cylinder car. The year 1912 also saw the company terminate production of their famous model "30," a popular, dependable line of almost six years' standing. Hereafter Packard was to devote its efforts exclusively to the six-, eight- and twelve-cylinder engines. A choice of 10 different body styles was offered on the 1912 "30" chassis with its wheelbase of 129½ inches. The close-coupled model owed its name to the designers' technique of coupling the front and rear seats relatively close to each other. Now it could accommodate only four passengers. However, to extend the seating capacity a "mother-in-law" seat was added at the rear. This unique appendage, introduced in 1909, evolved in later years into a rumble seat. Handsome fore-doors were placed on the driver's compartment and the panel forming the end of the front seat was curved in a pleasing tulip shape. A 40-h.p., four-cylinder engine of 5 × 5½" was standard on the "30." It also used a dry plate clutch, cellular radiator and an Eisemann low-tension magneto with step-up coil on the dash. Packard priced the close-coupled model at $4200.

## PLATE 89: Lozier Toy Tonneau, 1912

Lozier proudly advertised their 1912 line as "legitimately high priced." There is little doubt that the car had the credentials to back up this claim. The Detroit firm summarily dismissed all other competition with the flat statement that "the 1912 Lozier now holds all long distance American records, for road and speedway, regardless of class." Their 1912 Briarcliff toy tonneau, with its racy-looking cowl and aluminum body, was smartly styled, speedy and sold for $5500. Carpeted flooring, luxurious leather upholstery and brass-bound cork carpet mats at the driver's foot and toe board were installed in every car. The dashboard was particularly notable for its stark simplicity; only a door to the vibrator coil and an oil sight feed were placed on it. Two passengers could be seated in the 38-inch wide tonneau and, as an interesting innovation, there was a small seat on the running board. This was to be used by the chauffeur when the owner wished to drive. The 1912 Lozier catalog listed these specifications for their toy tonneaus: engine, six-cylinder, 51-h.p., 4⅝ × 5½" bore and stroke, valves on opposite sides; wheelbase, 131 inches; wheels, 36 × 4" front, 36 × 5" rear; transmission, four-speed selective type—direct on third. Speed in high, 60 mph and up.

## PLATE 90: American "22-B" Roadster, 1913

From 1905 to 1914 the American Motor Company of Indianapolis produced some of America's most unusual automobiles. They employed the highly imaginative design technique of turning the car's frame upside down; it was now slung under the axles rather than over them. In time this construction characteristic became so identified with the American car that the company officially named their product the American Underslung. While the "American Scout" roadster was the smallest, and cheapest, of the 1913 line, it still offered all the advantages of underslung construction. Its low center of gravity enabled it to hug the road almost as well as a racing car. Side slip and rear lash were reduced and the common tendency of most cars to sway at high speeds was practically eliminated. A more efficient, straight-line drive could be used

to transmit power, and higher wheels to add comfort were possible. The low-hung frame of the roadster also permitted the use of a low, rakish body. With a combination circular tire holder and luggage box, a 20-gallon gas tank and a road clearance of 9¾ inches, the roadster was well equipped for lengthy journeys over the hazardous roads of the day. It had a four-cylinder, 4" × 5" engine, measured 105 inches at the wheelbase and cost $1475.

## PLATE 91: Cadillac Coupé, 1913

In 1913 Cadillac won the internationally famed Dewar Trophy for the second time as a result of its pioneering in electrical starting, lighting and ignition. The self-starter was a milestone for the entire industry inasmuch as it served to double the number of potential drivers; now women could operate a car without the hazards of cranking. Another growing trend which was certain to capture the female eye was the smartly styled enclosed coupé. An increasing number of manufacturers of gasoline automobiles were beginning to challenge the electrics' hold on the market. The 1913 Cadillac coupé was an aluminum-bodied, four-passenger model billed as "a worthy companion" to the limousine. The driver's seat was hinged to permit easy entrance or exit from the right side; two passengers could be seated beside the driver and one in a drop seat. Hand-buffed leather upholstery trimmed with lace, silk curtains, dome light and a black-walnut hood shelf were only a few of its tasteful appointments. The rear and front quarter windows were stationary but the others could be lowered into pockets. The coupé body rode on a 120-inch wheelbase chassis and featured a four-cylinder, 40–50 horsepower engine. Its price was $2500.

## PLATE 92: Overland "69" Touring Car, 1913

The Overland four-cylinder car was almost as famous as Ford's Model T. Its guiding genius, John North Willys, had started as a bicycle seller in the 90's. He entered the Overland Company of Indianapolis as a salesman and soon became head of the organization. In 1909 he moved it to Toledo and in 1912 incorporated it as the Willys-Overland Company. His 1913 "69" touring car was an excellent piece of engineering and construction, superbly powered and handsomely styled. Its low price of $985 made it a bargain that few car makers of the day could match. One of its most advanced features was a ¾ floating rear axle capable of withstanding the severe punishment exerted by the roads of the day. It had powerful hub brakes of a contracting and expanding type, a cold-rolled steel frame and a mechanical oiler to lubricate cylinder walls and timing gears. The engine's four cylinders, set off center and measuring 4 × 4½", were single-cast with large water jackets. Upper and lower halves of the crank case were of aluminum construction. Some of the items which Overland included as standard equipment were: 3-ply mohair top, acetylene self-starter, gas lamps, robe rail, tire carrier in the rear and a full set of tools.

## PLATE 93: Peerless Roadster, 1913

The word "roadster" started appearing in the glossary of automotive body styles around 1906. Peerless was one of the first to use the term and by 1913 the company was producing a model whose neat, elegant styling and overall dash represents the roadster's development at one of its high-water marks. Its dome-shaped side lights set flat against the dash were a radical styling innovation. Control levers were all inside and doors fit flush with the body surface and in line with the top of the body. The windshield stays are well worth noting. Instead of slanting forward across the hood, they turned backward to the body parapet. The stays had a practical as well as aesthetic function; passengers entering the car could use them as grab handles. Sporting-minded motorists were particularly attracted to the roadster's handsome cape top and exposed rumble seat. An interesting mechanical air pump for inflating tires was included as standard equipment. It was driven by the motor. Mechanical specifications show these features: engine, six-cylinder, 4 × 5½" bore and stroke, 38 h.p.; ignition, Bosch, dual, magneto and battery; electric starter and lights; demountable rims with 36 × 4½" tires; brakes, contracting on rear wheels; 125-inch wheelbase; price, $4300, f.o.b. Cleveland.

## PLATE 94: Chevrolet Royal Mail Roadster, 1914

The story of "Fabulous Billy Durant" is one of the most colorful in the entire annals of the early auto industry. His meteoric rise to prominence as the prime mover in the affairs of the giant General Motors Corp. is well chronicled.

Somewhat less well known, however, is his participation in the founding of the Chevrolet Motor Company in 1911. Its first cars met with instantaneous success and by 1914 the demand for Chevrolets had not diminished. Two of the company's most famous models were sold in 1914—the Baby Grand Touring car and the Royal Mail Roadster. The roadster was a graceful-looking car, obviously designed and powered for buyers who wanted a dependable machine for ordinary day-to-day travel. Even though it was named after a famous racing driver, Louis Chevrolet, the car made no attempt to compete with some of the roadsters of the day whose trademarks were racy lines and blinding speed. It had a left-hand drive, flat rear deck with an oval 20-gallon gas tank, Zenith carburetor and acetylene headlights. The roadster carried a four-cylinder, valve-in-head, $3^{11}/_{16}'' \times 4''$ engine rated at 24 h.p. Wheelbase was 104 inches and its price, a modest $750.

## PLATE 95: Stutz Bearcat, 1914

The last Bearcat was made in the 1920s and fewer than 2000 were built. Yet the memory of this small, bucket-seated roadster with a dash and a zip all of its own is still vivid today. R. C. Stutz, its designer and builder, entered his first car in the 1911 Indianapolis "500." Its performance was so satisfying that he immediately adopted the slogan, "The car that made good in a day." The 1914 Bearcat had a wheelbase of 120 inches. Its only deviation from the other models of the year was its higher gear ratio and double-distributor Splitdorf magneto with two sets of plugs. Buyers had a choice of two T-Head Wisconsin motors, a four or a six, both with integral-head cast-iron blocks on an aluminum crankcase. Bore and stroke of the four-cylinder was $4^{3}/_{4}'' \times 5^{1}/_{2}''$; the six, $4 \times 5''$. Either would produce speeds up to 80 mph. A massive chassis was a feature of the car with half-elliptic springs all around. Electric starting and lighting, a 34-gallon gas tank and luggage trunk were standard equipment. Only three accessories were offered for the Bearcat in 1914: friction shock absorbers, wire wheels and Stewart or Warner speedometer. Price, f.o.b. Indianapolis: $2000 with four-cylinder engine, $2125 with the six.

## PLATE 96: Pierce-Arrow Vestibule Suburban, 1914

In 1914 Pierce-Arrow offered an amazing variety of 54 different bodies on their Series Three chassis. Each was a luxurious equipage that would have rivalled the finest product of the master coach builders of the 18th and 19th centuries. Those who were wealthy enough to purchase a Pierce-Arrow could choose from body styles ranging from a $4300 runabout to a seven-passenger landau costing $7200. The vestibule suburban, at $6200, sat on a 142-inch wheelbase and was equipped with a six-cylinder, $4^{1}/_{2} \times 5^{1}/_{2}''$, 48-horsepower engine. Its electric headlights mounted into the fender are well worth noting. This particular construction technique was patented by Pierce-Arrow and became a trademark of the car. Another interesting feature is the use of a right-hand drive at a time when most manufacturers were switching to left-hand steering. Pierce continued this arrangement until the early 1920s. One unsubstantiated theory holds that the right-hand position allowed chauffeurs to get to the sidewalk more quickly to open the door for madam. The Vestibule Suburban's rear door was domed for easier entry and its five-passenger rear compartment featured: dome and pillar lamps, a telephone to the chauffeur, a clock and frameless windows with regulators.

## PLATE 97: Chevrolet Baby Grand Touring Car, 1914

Frequently in the history of the early automotive industry a model would appear in which a happy blend of sound engineering and just the right styling approach would combine to produce a machine which far exceeded anything in its price class. The 1914 Chevrolet Baby Grand, companion model to the Royal Mail Roadster, was such an automobile. In that year Durant and his partners were able to sell every Chevrolet their Flint, Mich. plant could turn out. The Baby Grand's body was made of heavy-gauge metal with steel sills and doorposts. Doors were hung on recessed hinges and a gently curving cowl added to the car's overall streamline effect. The first four-cylinder overhead valve engines Chevrolet used were fitted on these models. They had a $3^{11}/_{16}'' \times 4''$ bore and stroke with a 24-h.p. rating. A one-inch, updraft Zenith

carburetor and a splash type lubrication system with oil pump were standard equipment. Other specifications: mechanical band brakes, rear wheels only; cone clutch; sliding spur gear type transmission; bevel drive gears, split axle housing; weight, 1975 pounds; wheelbase, 104 inches; price, $875. The name "Baby Grand" was not just a nickname for this model. It was an actual factory name, engraved on special plates.

## PLATE 98: Hupmobile "32" Touring Car, 1914

The demise of Hupmobile just prior to World War II marked the end of a long line of cars that had provided generations of Americans with steady, dependable transportation for many years. Though remembered primarily as a family-type car, Hupmobile featured many innovations; it also gave birth to such creations as the Cord-inspired Skylark. The original 1909 Hupmobile was named after its creator and designer, Robert C. Hupp. When this "32" touring model appeared in 1914, the company had dealerships throughout the U.S., a factory in Canada and a five-acre plant in Detroit. The "32" was instantly recognizable by its unique styling lines—a severely sloping hood and high-mounted gas headlights. The five-passenger touring car was placed on a 106-inch wheelbase and exhibited many refinements for its moderate price of $1050. Doors fitted flush with the body and hung on disappearing hinges; they had upholstered arms and pockets in the side walls. The rear compartment showed a luxurious cocoa mat on the floor. Other specifications: four-cylinder, "L"-head, $3^{1}/_{4} \times 5^{1}/_{2}''$ motor; left-hand drive; selective sliding transmission; direct-shaft drive; high-tension magneto ignition with single wiring system; water-cooling with extra-large, honeycomb type radiator.

## PLATE 99: Dodge Touring Car, 1914

Long before the famous car bearing the Dodge name was announced in 1914, John and Horace Dodge had built the vital parts for almost half a million cars in their Hamtramck plant. They were both completely loyal to their principal customer, Henry Ford, insisting that the Ford was the best piece of mechanism ever put on the American market for the money. However, they aimed at building an even better product. On November 14, 1914 the first Dodge car, a touring model, was adjudged ready for sale. In what little time remained of that first year, there were 249 Dodges produced and sold; the next year production skyrocketed to 45,033. The 1914-produced model boasted an all-steel body for the low price of $785. It had a 12-volt, 40-ampere battery for starter, lights and horn and featured a windshield which could be adjusted for "rain vision, clear vision and ventilating." Dodge Bros.' long experience in the motor industry was outstandingly evident in the simple, reliable engine they used. It was a 30–35 h.p., four-cylinder, L-Head type with bore and stroke of $3^{7}/_{8} \times 4^{1}/_{2}''$; top speed was 63 mph. Other specifications: selective sliding gear type transmission; 110 inch wheelbase; hickory wheels with demountable rims, $32 \times 3^{1}/_{2}''$ tires; Timken bearings throughout; weight, 2200 pounds.

## PLATE 100: Locomobile Town Coupé, 1915

In 1915 Locomobile confined production to only four cars a day. Their philosophy that "small numbers make for distinction . . . quantity destroys" is certainly alien to today's mass-production concepts. It did, however, lead to the creation of some of the most elegant and luxurious cars ever turned out by American automakers. The two-passenger town coupé was designed and built by Locomobile in its own custom body department. Everything about the car—from its huge, six-inch, chrome-nickel alloy steel frame to its cut-glass sidelamps, jewel-like in detail—was impressive. Its wheelbase of 140 inches was one of the largest of the day and 40-inch springs in the front, 50- in the rear, provided an unusually easy ride. A powerful six-cylinder engine of $4^{1}/_{2} \times 5^{1}/_{2}''$ carried an actual horsepower rating of slightly over 82. Electric starting and lighting, two-jet carburetion, four-speed transmission and full floating rear axle were only a few of the town coupé's notable features. Leading authorities on interior decoration were consulted to insure that the passenger's rear compartment was finished in unquestioned taste. Fine fabrics were lavished on it along with delicately inlaid wood vanity cases, silk roller shades and a French type telephone concealed in a specially designed compartment.

# Index of Plates

Abbott-Detroit "30" Roadster (1912), 87
Alco Touring Car (1911), 80
American "22-B" Roadster (1913), 90
Apperson Touring Car (1907), 59
Autocar Phaeton (1898), 20
Autocar Runabout (1906), 54
Black Gasoline Carriage (1893), 11
Brewster Limousine (1911), 79
Buick "G" Runabout (1907), 60
Buick "10" Toy Tonneau (1910), 75
Buick "26" Runabout (1911), 81
Cadillac Coupé (1913), 91
Cadillac "D" Touring Car (1905), 51
Cadillac "H" Limousine (1907), 62
Cadillac "M" Touring Car (1906), 57
Cadillac Tonneau (1903), 43
Carhart Steam Wagon (1871), 3
Chalmers-Detroit Coupé (1910), 73
Chevrolet Baby Grand Touring Car (1914), 97
Chevrolet Royal Mail Roadster (1914), 94
Columbia Daumon Victoria (1899), 26
Columbia Electric Phaeton (1900), 31
Copeland Steam Tricycle (1886), 5
Dodge Touring Car (1914), 99
Dudgeon Steam Wagon (1853), 1
Duryea Gasoline Buggy (1893), 10
Duryea Motor Wagon (1895), 15
Duryea Phaeton (1902), 35
Ford "A" Tonneau (1903), 44
Ford "B" Touring Car (1905), 49
Ford Gasoline Carriage (1898), 22
Ford "K" Touring Car (1906), 53
Ford Model "T" Touring Car (1909), 68
Ford Quadricycle (1896), 16
Franklin Runabout (1902), 37
Haynes-Apperson Surrey (1901), 32
Haynes Gasoline Carriage (1894), 12
Holsman Surrey (1905), 50
Holzer-Cabot Electric (1895), 14
Hudson Roadster (1910), 72
Hupmobile "32" Touring Car (1914), 98
King Horseless Carriage (1896), 17
Knox "M" Limousine (1909), 70
Knox Three-Wheeler (1899), 28
Lambert Gasoline Buggy (1891), 8
Locomobile Steamer (1899), 27
Locomobile Tonneau De Luxe (1904), 46
Locomobile Town Coupé (1915), 100
Lozier Toy Tonneau (1912), 89
Marmon "D" Touring Car (1906), 55

Matheson Toy Tonneau (1911), 83
Maxwell Tourabout (1907), 58
Mercer Raceabout (1911), 84
Morris & Salom Electrobat (1895), 13
Morrison-Sturgis Electric (1890), 6
Mueller Motor Carriage (1897), 18
Nadig Road Wagon (1891), 7
Oakland "K" Touring Car (1910), 78
Oldsmobile "A" Touring Car (1907), 63
Oldsmobile Curved Dash Runabout (1903), 45
Olds Motor Carriage (1897), 19
Overland "69" Touring Car (1913), 92
Packard Berline (1910), 76
Packard "F" Tonneau (1902), 36
Packard Model "A" (1899), 25
Packard "S-24" Victoria (1906), 56
Packard "30" Close-Coupled (1912), 88
Peerless Roadster (1913), 93
Peerless Touring Car (1903), 42
Pierce-Arrow Vestibule Suburban (1914), 96
Pierce Great Arrow Touring Car (1908), 65
Pope-Waverley "60-A" Surrey (1907), 61
Rambler Landaulet (1911), 85
Rambler Runabout (1902), 38
Rambler Tonneau (1904), 47
Rauch & Lang Brougham (1908), 66
Reo Roadster (1910), 74
Riker Electric Brougham (1900), 29
Riker Electric Tricycle (1898), 24
Riker Theater Bus (1901), 33
Roper Steam Carriage (1863), 2
S. & M. Simplex Limousine (1907), 64
Schloemer-Toepfer Carriage (1892), 9
Sears Motor Buggy (1910), 77
Selden Road Wagon (1877), 4
Simplex Speedster (1912), 86
Stanley Roadster (1908), 67
Stanley Steamer (1902), 39
Stearns "40–45" Limousine (1906), 52
Studebaker "A" Suburban (1909), 69
Studebaker Electric Runabout (1902), 40
Studebaker Touring Car (1904), 48
Stutz Bearcat (1914), 95
Thomas Flyer Touring Car (1909), 71
White Steamer (1901), 34
White "30" Landaulet (1911), 82
Winton Motor Carriage (1898), 23
Winton Touring Car (1903), 41
Woods Electric Hansom (1898), 21
Woods Station Wagon (1900), 30